John D. Forsyth

THE AGGIES AND THE 'HORNS

THE AGGIES AND THE 'HORNS

BY
JOHN D. FORSYTH

Texas Monthly Press

Texas Monthly Press, Inc.
P. O. Box 1569
Austin, Texas 78767

A   B   C   D   E   F   G   H

Forsyth, John D., 1953–
    The Aggies and the 'Horns.

    Bibliography: p.
    1. Texas A & M University—History.
2. University of Texas at Austin—History.
I. Title.
LD5309.F67   378.764′31   81-8922
ISBN 0-932012-14-0

Book Design by Sagebrush Studio
Book Production by The Composing Stick

Thanks to
The late James M. "Cop" Forsyth
(Texas A&M '12).
Also to
Frank G. Anderson
Herschel E. Burgess
Julie DelCour Cleary
Spec Gammon
Mike Nichols
Arno "Shorty" Nowotny
David A. Wright

For my parents

THE AGGIES AND THE 'HORNS

Beat the Hell Out of Texas

By Billy Clayton
Speaker, Texas House of Representatives

It's about time somebody got around to chronicling the football history of Texas A&M and the University of Texas. It was on the playing field that the rivalry between the two schools began, and it is the battles of the playing field that keeps the rivalry at a fever pitch, year in and year out. It isn't likely that either of the schools would ever have a winless season, but if ever either or both did, it wouldn't make any difference the day they play.

The A&M–UT clash is the game of the year in both College Station and Austin. Toss out the statistics, forget the win-loss record, concentrate on how to not only beat, but humble, humiliate, and annihilate the opponent. There is nothing that gets the Aggie juices flowing better than to "saw Varsity's horns off." There is nothing more pleasant than to see all of that orange blood drain slowly from tortured faces. There is nothing to compare with watching those once-proud hand signs turn to quivering jelly.

Those among us fortunate enough to have learned the A&M tradition from square one know the most important words in any Aggie's vocabulary, the unwritten eleventh commandment and, most assuredly, a sound even Mozart could not sweeten: "Beat the Hell out of Texas." After all, what more could an Aggie be thankful for if they make turkeys out of the Longhorns on Thanksgiving Day. And those urban cowboys routinely have as much trouble with the Aggies as they do walking barefoot behind their old cow. They may be able to clean their feet, but they'll never get the Aggies off their backs.

When it comes time to talk about college days, it's time for Aggies to talk about how they fared against the Tea-Sips. Whether at the Dixie Chicken or in the board rooms of giant Texas corporations, the Monday morning talk during late autumn concerns how the Aggies fared and what the stats mean in the scope of life—how will all this affect us when we play the 'Horns.

On the field of play or off, there is something fulfilling about the adage that the best always rises to the top—the cream on the milk, the grain and not the chaff. They can call the Aggies country bumpkins and make all kinds of jokes, but we all know what they call an Aggie a few years after graduation—Boss.

John Forsyth did all of us Aggies a big favor by writing about our big wins. It would have been fine to have misplaced a few of the games—but on balance we wouldn't have had it any other way, especially after three in a row.

Ma-Ma, Da-Da, and Hook 'Em 'Horns

By Lloyd Doggett
State Senator, District 14

Those of us whose blood runs orange are willing to discuss at great length the natural superiority of the "University of the First Class," located in Austin, to that strange institution, situated on the south pasture out of Bryan, which trains veterinarians and county agents. Everyone knows that UT represents urban sophistication, while A&M represents a bucolic America that is rapidly passing from the scene. Even the Aggie pejorative term for Longhorns, "Tea-Sips," indicates that *they* recognize **The University** as a place for culture and good taste.

What is it that makes adult Texans, long ago separated from the college campus, square off with a passion more intense than that which separates Republicans from Democrats, Hatfields from McCoys, or the Mafia from the FBI? What is it that makes a large portion of the adult population of the southwestern United States tell and/or laugh at Aggie jokes with a glee that surpasses that reserved for any other kind of humor? It is a rivalry unsurpassed among Americans, a rivalry that could only happen on the edge of the Last Frontier where people really know how to hold a grudge. Harvard vs. Yale, Army vs. Navy, Alabama vs. Auburn—they pale by comparison.

It is on the football field that the rivalry reaches its zenith. Four generations of Texans have grown up on Thanksgiving Day with fried chicken or tuna fish sandwiches eaten in a parking lot in Austin or a cow pasture in College Station. Who would prefer turkey and dressing and Pilgrims to gladiators in burnt orange and scrawny but tenacious farmers in maroon? Those unfortunates who didn't make it to the playing field clung to their radios, in the early days, or their televisions, lately, and gobbled their candied yams and cranberry sauce, dribbled the orange and maroon impartially on their chests, and dared anyone to insinuate that giving thanks for America's blessings was anywhere near as important as listening to the Longhorns embarrass the Aggies. In the late seventies, when **The Game** was moved from Thanksgiving Thursday, a new generation had to learn what the fourth Thursday in November was supposed to be about, and that the battle was just as intense no matter when it was staged.

It is a rivalry based on what was at one time a real difference in outlook—with UT representing urban Texas and A&M representing rural Texas at a time when the state was much more evenly divided along those lines. Through the years the real differences have faded, but all the trappings have assumed centrality, and the rivalry sustains itself year after year.

And so we move along. We teach our children at the earliest age possible to raise their index finger and little finger in the famous (or infamous) sign and to say, right after "Ma-Ma" and "Da-Da," "Hook 'em 'Horns!"

The remembrances that are brought to life here, even those few that are painful, make the orange blood rush.

1890'S

1894

The Opening Salvo

The University of Texas' 1894 football team needed a practice game before its first interstate battle, an October game with Tulane. A scrimmage squad was rounded up at Texas Agricultural & Mechanical College and hauled to Austin. Thus began the Southwest's fiercest sporting rivalry.

The first game of American football, between Rutgers and Princeton, had been history for twenty-four years when UT fielded its first official team in 1893. Already the sport had undergone numerous transformations since its birth as a rugby-like affair in 1869, but the rules changes hadn't lessened its inherent roughness. It was a brutal game indeed that Texas entered with a $100 football budget.

Schools in the East remained the power bloc of gridiron might, although the universities of Michigan and Chicago were showing strength. The Wolverines had shown Notre Dame how to play the game back in 1887, the same year in which the first system of

downs had been installed, allowing a team to retain possession of the ball only if it gained five yards in three downs. Reward for a touchdown was four points and a conversion two.

Mass momentum plays such as Harvard's "Flying Wedge," which positioned the ball carrier behind a "V" of blockers, were popular among schools with weight on their side. Such tactics often turned an opponent's personnel roster into a list of those wounded in action.

It would prove typical of Texas' football history that the team went undefeated its first year. Its only foes in 1893 were the Dallas Foot Ball Club and San Antonio High School, but the 4–0 record against the two teams would represent only the first of ten undefeated and untied teams over eighty-seven years at Austin.

Before the Tulane game in 1894, the first encounter of Texas' season, the university sent W. O. Stephens, one of its players, to College Station to organize a team at A&MC and bring it back to Austin for the slaughter. Stephens told an Austin reporter about it in 1926.

A&MC's squad had warmed up with a

14–6 victory over Galveston High School, so both schools owned unblemished football histories when they produced the state's first intercollegiate football game in suburban Austin's Hyde Park. A playing area had been roped off; one dollar was charged for admission.

A&MC fumbled the opening kickoff and Texas scored in two plays. Texas eventually chalked up 38 points to A&MC's 0. For the boys from College Station, the season was over at one win, one loss. The university, however, notched five more shutout victories (including 12–0 over Tulane) before its final game of the year, in which Missouri stopped Texas' two-year, never-been-beaten streak at ten games. ●

1898

Killing with Kindness

A&MC didn't come up with a team in 1895, and when it did in 1896 and 1897, Texas wasn't on its schedule. In Austin, however, football enthusiasts had a lot to

Frank Dudley Perkins (with ball) *coached A&MC's first football team to a 38–0 slaughter in Austin, 1894.*

The 1896 Aggie team piled up a 2–0–1 record, but Texas was not among its opponents again until 1898.

A former Missouri end, Horace W. Williams became head coach at A&M in 1898.

holler about. Texas' teams went 5–0, 4–2–1, and 6–2 after 1894.

The sport continued to change. Some of the dangerous mass momentum plays, characteristic of a street brawl, had been outlawed in 1896. But football players, without benefit of helmet or padding, still put their health on the line for "one of the greatest games of the 19th century." One A&MC-ex put it this way:

> Went to see the football game,
> Thought that I could play the same,
> So in haste I joined the 'leven—
> I am writing this from Heaven.

A&MC took seventeen players to Austin's Athletic Park on a Saturday in October, 1898, and they outweighed Texas' team by fifteen pounds per man. Seventy-five cadets went along as a cheering section, equipped with cowbells, sleighbells, and foghorns.

Kicking was a dominant weapon in the game's early years. Teams did not like to find themselves with the ball deep in their own end of the field, so punting, even on first down, was common. Under a revised scoring system, a placekick through the goalposts, following a five-point touchdown, was worth one point; a field goal accounted for four points. The *Austin Statesman* reported, however, that Texas showed a weak-

The Farmers' first salaried coach, C. W. Taylor, saw his 1897 team lose the season opener, then go on to defeat TCU and Austin College.

ness where its goal-kicking game was concerned: "When a 'Varsity man attempts to kick one of those blasted goals, it is on the order of a girl throwing a rock, much safer to be behind than in any other direction."

Rough play and fumbles again were common in the game. A&MC's quarterback, H. H. Tracey, was the recipient of several hard blows on the stomach and head and was knocked cold, placed on a wagon, and taken downtown to receive medical attention. The entire A&MC team must have felt the same way, for the final score was 48–0 in favor of Texas. The score remains the most lopsided defeat ever suffered by an Aggie team.

Still, the Farmers felt they had been treated royally during their stay in the city and thanked the 'Varsity boys for their many kind acts. ●

1899

Nothing Like a Graceful Loser

By the close of the century, both the university and A&MC had begun to show some muscle among teams in the South. In 1899, each would defeat Tulane and Louisiana State and give Tennessee's tough Sewanee Indian School a close game. (Sewanee beat five teams in six days on a 3,000-mile trip through Texas, Louisiana, and Mississippi.)

The Farmer backfield of 1899 includes (left to right): Charley Johnson, halfback, Earle "Dutch" Schultz, fullback, Frank Dwyer, halfback, and O. M. Simpson, quarterback.

Even the bare minimum seemed luxurious to cadets who rated rooms at A&MC at the turn of the century.

1899

Texas also would allow powerhouse Vanderbilt to escape with only a 6–0 decision.

Still, football in the South wasn't recognized as football the way schools in the East and the Midwest played it. Yale, Harvard, Princeton, and Pennsylvania held sway on the coast. Amos Alonzo Stagg's University of Chicago Maroons had been a steamroller for years. When football innovator and authority Walter Camp selected his All-America teams, he only rarely considered players outside the Eastern bloc and never looked as far as the Southwest. Neither A&M nor Texas would have an All-America representative for more than thirty-five years.

Despite the interstate opportunities to make good showings, Texas and A&MC already considered their battle with each other the highlight of each season: the state championship was always at stake. So it was with great eagerness that the Farmers looked toward the 1899 game with 'Varsity. The boys from College Station easily had their best team to date. Apart from their loss to Sewanee, A&MC had vanquished four foes by a total 150–0. One student let his feelings be known in somewhat irregular verse in *The Battalion*, A&MC's student publication:

'Varsity, 'Varsity,
Who are they?
Surely not state champion,
For wait till you see AMC.

But the Farmers needed more than poetry. They needed a touchdown or two. Texas, coached by hard-nosed Huston Thompson, held the potent A&MC offense scoreless while earning six points en route to its third win in a 5–2 season. But the game, played in San Antonio, ended in dispute. When Texas was awarded possession at the Farmer's two-yard line after a wild scramble for a fumble, A&MC Captain Hal Moseley led his team off the field with twenty-eight minutes to play. The Farmers literally took their ball and went home. ●

1900'S

1900

Close and Less Close

Their walkout the previous year notwithstanding, the Farmers came back for more and lined up two games with Texas in 1900. Again, the A&MC players considered themselves ready. Coach W. A. Murray pushed his troops hard in his second year at the college. And at 6'3" and 200 pounds he was considered the man to do it. In their first game, his boys held highly respected Kansas City Medical College to a 6–6 deadlock.

Texas, however, had opened its decades-long argument with Oklahoma with a 28–2 victory and had handed tough Vanderbilt a 22–0 setback. When the state's arch enemies met in October before 1,200 rooters at San Antonio's muddy fair grounds, at least the strategies resembled those of two of the Eastern giants. Texas employed quick plunges into the line and rapid darts around end—out of Princeton's play book. A&MC emulated Pennsylvania with its "guards back" and other heavy mass plays against the line and through the tackles. A single touchdown gave the Austinites their narrowest win

W. A. Murray progressed from captain of Penn State's 1898 team to coach at A&M from 1899 to 1901.

THE RESULTS OF AN ELECTION CONDUCTED DURING THE FIRST HALF OF 1953 BY STUDENTS ATTENDING TEXAS A & M COLLEGE PRIOR TO DEC. 31, 1900, IN WHICH ABOUT THIRTY PER-CENT OF THOSE CONTACTED PARTICIPATED, PLACED THESE AGGIES ON THE FIRST, SECOND AND THIRD MYTHICAL FOOTBALL TEAMS TO REPRESENT THE DECADE ENDING DEC. 31, 1900

FIRST TEAM

SPONSOR	MRS. MARY H. NELSON	'03	NEW ORLEANS, LA.
L. E.	F. K. McGINNIS	'00	TERRELL, TEX.
L. T.	HAL W. MOSELEY	'00	DALLAS, TEX.
L. G.	CHAS. BAUMGARTEN	'99	SCHULENBURG, TEX.
C.	R. B. BOETTCHER	'00	WEIMAR, TEX.
R. G.	ARTHUR WEINERT	'00	SEGUIN, TEX.
R. T.	E. H. ASTIN	'99	BRYAN, TEX.
R. E.	J. B. STERNS	'99	HOUSTON, TEX.
Q. B.	H. H. TRACY	'98	OAK CLIFF, TEX.
H. B.	R. M. BROWN	'01	AUSTIN, TEX.
F. B.	W. F. DWYER	'99	SAN MARCOS, TEX.
H. B.	H. E. RAWLINS	'98	OAK CLIFF, TEX.

SECOND TEAM

SPONSOR	MRS. MARY BITTLE TODD		BRYAN, TEX.
L. E.	R. W. COUSINS	'99	AUSTIN, TEX.
L. T.	J. D. THROWER	'00	MAYHEW, MISS.
L. G.	O. W. MYERS	'00	JOSEPHINE, TEX.
C.	E. M. OVERSHINER	'97	VALLEY VIEW, TEX.
R. G.	H. H. UECKERT	'98	REINHARDT, TEX.
R. T.	T. H. GARRETT	'01	MART, TEX.
R. E.	A. C. LOVE	'99	FRANKLIN, TEX.
Q. B.	O. M. SIMPSON	'00	JACKSBORO, TEX.
H. B.	E. C. SCHULTZ	'04	TRINITY, TEX.
F. B.	F. D. PERKINS	'97	McKINNEY, TEX.
H. B.	ROBERT RAGSDALE	'99	HALLETTSVILLE, TEX.

HONORABLE MENTION

SPONSOR	MISS ETHEL CAVITT		BRYAN, TEX.
L. E.	H. FOSTER	'01	COLLEGE STATION, TEX.
L. T.	R. W. BURLESON	'95	SAN SABA, TEX.
L. G.	P. G. KILDOW	'00	IOWA PARK, TEX.
C.	ANDREW WINKLER	'00	THE GROVE, TEX.
R. G.	J. W. BURNEY	'96	KERRVILLE, TEX.
R. T.	P. M. MORRISON	'97	GREENVILLE, TEX.
R. E.	WALTER HYDE	'02	TAYLOR, TEX.
Q. B.	W. G. MASSENBURG	'95	PARIS, TEX.
H. B.	H. T. COULTER	'95	BRYAN, TEX.
F. B.	RESO FARR	'98	BELTON, TEX.
H. B.	M. W. SIMS	'94	BRYAN, TEX.

A plaque honors the 1894–1900 All-Aggie team.

ever over A&MC, 5–0.

Revenge was on the minds of a trainload of A&MC players and rooters who arrived in Austin (population 22,258) in November. Rain at the 10:45 a.m. kickoff limited the crowd to about 700 for the schools' first Thanksgiving Day encounter. One onlooker from College Station got a little overzealous in his cheering, and a Texas player took after him. The cadet was removed from the scene after a brief fight.

Since they had last seen the Farmers, the 'Varsity players, clad this year (for the first time officially) in orange and white, had edged Missouri and had done surgery on the Kansas City Meds. They proceeded to sew up their third undefeated and untied season with an 11–0 decision over the Brazos boys, who could only watch as the hometown crowd lifted heroes onto shoulders and carried them downtown to a rally. Coach Murray would have two more shots at 'Varsity.

Captain M. T. Thomas, 1st Lieutenant Charley Kleinsmith, 2d Lieutenant E. B. Fehrenkamp (left to right) exhibit corps attire, circa 1900.

1901

The Beating Goes On

Before the start of the 1901 football season, the faculty at A&MC ruled that the school couldn't participate in intercollegiate athletics. There was a foul taste in the mouths of some over football's continued violence and the general disregard for player eligibility standards. But the order was rescinded after vigorous student protest.

Support for the rule might have been smarter. The school had a down year under W. A. Murray, a winless one if you side with Baylor University's record book. A&M still considers its 1901 opener a 6–0 victory over the Bears, but Baylor maintains that the score was 6–6. There's no quarrel over the result of a second Farmer-Bruin duel that year (Baylor won it, 17–6) or a third, after A&MC had played 'Varsity twice (Baylor won again, 46–0).

Compared with the Farmers' five-game season, Texas was busy and successful, going 8–2–1 for the year. Neither loss was to the school at College Station. The Texas-Farmer games remained the highlight of college athletics in the state, as *The Houston Post* reported: "Evolution of Texas football centers around and is bound up in her two greatest institutions." The university was greater again in 1901, and pummeled the college twice, 17–0 and 32–0.

The fifth season of the rivalry coincided with an oddity on the national scene. The Lost Rose Bowl is memorable today because it was so long forgotten. Neither Texas nor A&MC played in the first Rose Bowl in Pasadena, California, of course. Michigan did, much to Stanford's chagrin. Chariot races had carried the January 1 Rose Bowl Parade for years, but festival officials sought a new event. The 1901 Stanford Cardinals had carved an impressive record and a post-season game was envisioned purely to showcase the local boys' football talent. When Michigan accepted the invitation to fill the visitor's role, plans were set. The Wolverines suffocated the Cardinals, 49–0, on New Year's Day in 1902, and snuffed out the budding Rose Bowl in the process. The parade fathers were so humiliated that they returned to chariot races for the next fourteen Rose Bowl parades. Stanford was so embarrassed, too, that it temporarily quit football.

1902

Aggies Hallelujah!

Stopping the seven-game losing streak at the hands of 'Varsity became more important than ever during A&MC's 1902 season. Again the Farmers' schedule listed Texas twice, in their fifth and ninth games.

The Farmers were 3–0–1 against other state foes going into the first game with Texas, which stood 2–1 with impressive wins over Sewanee and Oklahoma. A few hundred A&MC cadets rode freight cars to San Antonio for the game. The weather was ideal, with a little breeze and slightly cool temperatures. For the first time in the series, neither team scored. Fumbles ended two Texas drives deep in A&MC territory. The 0–0 deadlock dented 'Varsity's domination of the Farmers, but A&MC's boys took little solace in the tie.

Ten school officials gathered in 1901 to form the University of Texas Athletic Council. A decade later, the Council would vote to scratch A&MC from their playing schedule.

Dutch Schultz models an early look in football gear. Although padding was slight and helmets weren't yet standard equipment, some players wore face guards.

The farmers trample St. Edwards at College Station in the opening game of the 1902 season, the first of two 11–0 victories over Austin schools that year.

Texas had outscored A&MC 157–0 in fashioning a 6–0–1 all-time record against its No. 1 enemy. The Farmers weren't alone in losing to Texas. Tulane was 0–6 against the Austin school by this time, and had scored 4 points to 'Varsity's 89. Arkansas was on its way toward losing its first twelve games to Texas, the first ten by an aggregate score of 263–6. Trinity's first five games with Texas would amount to a 0–126 scorecard.

The Saturday before the second game with Texas, A&MC coach J. E. Platt sent one of his players, Josh Sterns, to Austin to study 'Varsity's game. The first use of a football scout in the state proved profitable, for on November 27, a cool Thanksgiving Day, history took a turn in favor of the Farmers. They scored two touchdowns while holding Texas pointless. By virtue of its season-ending 11–0 win, the college laid claim to the championship of the South, as Sewanee had downed the previously unbeaten Commodores of Vanderbilt.

1903

Horns and "Eyes"

Alex Weisburg, editor-in-chief of *The Texan*, gave sportswriter D. A. Frank an order. "D. A.," Weisburg instructed, "hereafter in every sports article call the team 'The Longhorns' and we'll soon have it named." In relating the tale years later, Frank said those instructions were passed down for a few years, and "along about 1906 or 1907 the name became official."

The newly dubbed warriors horned in on a number of folks, suffering their only loss at the hands of Oklahoma's Haskell Indian School. Texas stood 4–1–2 before the Farmer game, and A&MC was 6–2–1. But records mattered little. The previous year's 'Varsity squad was the first to lose to the college, so there was a debt to be paid. A&MC

cashed in a Texas fumble four minutes after the opening kickoff for a 6–0 lead. But Texas quickly eliminated any suspense in the fumble-sprinkled contest and withdrew a 29–6 decision in Austin. The Farmers' victory of a year earlier had served only to inflate the rivalry.

1903 was also notable for Texas fans because the song, "The Eyes of Texas," was written that year by John Lang Sinclair, who wrote it for a minstrel show as a satire on Dr. Lambdin Prather, the university's president. Prather had attended Washington and Lee University when General Robert E. Lee was its president. It was said that Lee always noted in his addresses to the students that "the eyes of the South are upon you." Prather often quoted the saying, confining it to Texas eyes; it soon became a standing joke among the Texas student body. At the minstrel show, the song (sung to the tune of "I've Been Working on the Railroad") became a tremendous hit and was sung far into the night. Gradually, it

'Varsity roster from the 1903 Cactus.

The Eyes of Texas

The Eyes of Texas are upon you,
All the livelong day.
The Eyes of Texas are upon you,
You cannot get away.
Do not think you can escape them,
At night or early in the morn,
The Eyes of Texas are upon you
Till Gabriel blows his horn.

"The Eyes of Texas," written in 1903 by John Lang Sinclair, appears as the school song in the 1912 Cactus.

Don "Mogul" Robinson played fullback on Texas' 1903–1905 teams, earned a place on the All-Southwest Conference team for the first half-century of college football.

became the school song and unofficial song of the state. ●

the game was called at dark, they were down 34–6. ●

one year's residence, maintain a fifteen-hour work load, be eligible only four years, and receive no pay for play. ●

1904

No Place Like Home

Up to 1904, the games the two teams played prior to the Texas-A&MC encounter were viewed as mere curtain raisers before a championship prize fight. This wasn't so in 1904.

Texas chose that year to schedule its first game against a major Midwest power. The University of Chicago was in the midst of winning all but seven games from 1902 to 1909, and was at the very peak of its power when Texas issued its challenge. The Maroons' legendary coach, Amos Alonzo Stagg, seemingly invented most of the modern game. A typical example of Stagg's brilliance would come a year later, when the forward pass was legalized and Stagg immediately incorporated sixty-four pass patterns into his schemes, including the "guard eligible" and the "shoe-string" or "sleeper" to the sideline.

The 1904 'Varsity gridders were 2–1 upon taking the train to St. Louis, where they bludgeoned Washington University 23–0 and took in the World's Fair. But the pigskin didn't bounce so readily in their direction a couple of days later at Stagg Field. Chicago's incomparable Walter Eckersley returned a Texas fumble 100 yards for a touchdown early on to initiate the flood. Not only were the visitors drowned in the ensuing 68–0 torrent, so was Southwestern football's burgeoning reputation. The pain of Texas' wound suffered in Chicago remained fierce, but no Longhorn team would ever get a shot at revenge. Chicago gave up the sport in 1940 without having faced Texas again.

Texas recovered to paddle Oklahoma, 40–10, and Baylor, 58–0, before facing the Farmers. A&MC's season had been comparatively lackluster. Their 4–1 ledger had been compiled against weak teams. Still, there was a hint of state championship in the annual Texas shootout.

Temperance champion Carrie Nation was on hand to preach to the Austin crowd against the brutality of football. Hours later, the Farmers would be in agreement. When

1905

"Genuine Students"

During the fall of 1905, Texas suffered a record four defeats, and A&M stomped seven of its first eight opponents. It was easily 'Varsity's worst season of football. The Farmers had been stopped only by Transylvania College of Kentucky, and were favored in the Texas game.

The cadets' battle cry was "Remember 1902—11–0!" Texas gave them something else to remember, a 27–0 setback. It was the first year of five over the decades in which a defeat of Texas A&M enabled Texas to avoid a losing season. They were lucky to have future chances; football was on the ropes in 1905.

"Death and injuries are not the strongest argument against football . . . that cheating and brutality are profitable is the main evil." This pronouncement came from the president of Harvard, Dr. Charles W. Eliot. There were a record twenty-four football-related deaths that year.

"Clean it up," said President Teddy Roosevelt, and the elder statesmen of the sport would heed his words. Roosevelt considered it a losing season for everyone because of the mortality rate. The rulemakers could do nothing to slow the "profitable" betting attendant at most games; their alterations, to be implemented in 1906, took aim at the game's injurious nature. Among the new guidelines were the establishment of a neutral zone at the line of scrimmage, elimination of the remaining mass momentum plays, extension of the first-down requirement to ten yards in four downs (which A&M's *Battalion* had urged as early as 1894), and approval of the forward pass. Wholesale acceptance of the pass remained nearly a decade away.

Roosevelt also sought standards for player eligibility. A professor at Harvard drew up a list of rules, including one stating that "all members of teams [must] be 'genuine students' of the university and satisfactory in the studies." University of Pennsylvania officials offered several guidelines: that a player have

1906

"Slow as Mud"

At Texas Agricultural and Mechanical College, the earliest football games were played on the drill field. Spectators sat in carriages or stood around the field. Some games were staged at the fair grounds in Bryan. The school's first stadium came into being when E. J. Kyle, chairman of the athletic council, ordered a section of agricultural land fenced in 1904. The grandstands at the fair grounds were purchased and moved to the site, offering relative comfort to 500.

The captain of the 1906 'Varsity team, Lucian Parrish, proudly wears his letter sweater.

Fenced in 1904, Kyle Field was further improved with the addition of grandstands in 1906.

'Varsity hadn't played in College Station before 1904, and they wouldn't until 1915. All A&M-Texas games had been in San Antonio or Austin. This created part of the hostility that emanated from College Station and would be a major argument used by A&M in discussions to establish a Southwestern athletic conference.

Another force fanning the dislike between the two teams involved personal opinions. The facilities at A&M were somewhat limited, and many of the cadets lived in large army tents. This added to the cadets' reputation as roughnecks among the students at Austin. An

ex-A&M official would put it more succinctly years later: "They hated us." In perfect opposition, the cadets regarded the university crowd as sissies.

Individually, A&M and Texas played good football under the new rules of 1906. The Farmers' season was not blemished by a loss in six games prior to the big one, and they had outscored their opponents by 170–18. Texas' 177–15 mastery of eight foes eclipsed its single loss, a 45–0 torture session at the hands of mighty Vanderbilt. On Thanksgiving afternoon before an Austin crowd of about 4,000, the Commodores were forgotten. The

Eyes of Texas were upon the Farmers of Texas A&MC.

Cadet chants of "Hullaballoo" and "Rattle-de-thrat" sounded throughout the contest, but A&M's players appeared unmoved by the spirit. As a matter of fact, they hardly moved at all, according to *The Texan*'s report of the clash. The paper critiqued the opponents' play bluntly: "The Farmers were slow as mud." Fred Ramsdell of the home team was anything but slow, carrying the ball for nearly 200 yards in a 24–0 decision, the college's only loss for the year. ●

1907

Hard Times

A Texas team traveled to Dallas for its first season-opener with Texas A&M since 1894. Circus cars congested the track and delayed the team's train. Team captain Bowie Duncan employed the occasion to promise revenge for the loss suffered by his brother Vance's squad back in 1902.

Team captain for the Farmers was the great halfback Joe Utay. He would become, in 1974, the first Southwest pioneer player to be named to the National Football Hall of Fame, but he would never beat Texas. In the Dallas game, the result was the second 0–0 tie in the rivalry's history. Texas had completed its bleachers at Austin's Clark Field for the Thanksgiving encounter, so spectators no longer pushed in to stand along a barbed wire fence. When the cadets arrived, they were in high spirits, for their team remained undefeated for this season finale. They put their joy to song:

> Oh, we come here on Thanksgiving Day
> To see if 'Varsity has learned how to play;
>   And it's hard times at Var-si-tee.
> They look awful big but guess what it is?
> A big pile of mush, a whole lotta fizz;
>   And it's hard times at Var-si-tee.
> Just what they are we really don't care;
> They're puffed up and blown up and filled with hot air
>   And it's hard times at Var-si-tee.
> And if they don't beat us they always get mad,
> And then they try to fight. O my. Ain't they bad?
>   And it's hard times at Var-si-tee.

All the scoring was registered in the first half. A&M recovered a fumble deep in 'Varsity territory to take a 6–5 lead. Then Fred Ramsdell, the Farmers' nemesis of a year earlier, carried an interception forty yards for a touchdown. The Longhorns won, 11–6, and it was Hard Times at A&MC.

1908

"Lose to Everybody Else"

The cross-state rivalry really heated up in its twelfth season. Both schools fielded comparatively weak teams, but past accomplishments or failures rarely affected the outcome of the A&M-Texas game, leaving the dopesters stumped. One week before the A&M game, the Longhorns sustained the most ignominious loss in their history. Southwestern University in Georgetown, Texas, a school that "didn't know a football from a toy balloon," popped the 'Varsity with an 11–9 verdict.

Houston's No-Tsu-Oh Carnival (No-Tsu-Oh is *Houston* spelled backwards), a wild weekend of festivities at West End Park, pro-

Despite never having defeated Texas, 1907 team captain Joe Utay (holding ball) *became the first Southwest pioneer player to be named to the National Football Hall of Fame.*

Farmers practice in front of Foster Hall, circa 1908.

vided a tense environment for the first of 1908's two A&M-Texas clashes. The Texas band had to omit a yell with the word *hell* in it from its repertoire before it was allowed to attend. But the band let the cadets know how things stood (to the tune of taps): "A&M, A&M, Soak your head and go to bed." The playing, presumably, was better than the lyric.

Texas rooters staged an "interhalf parade" on the field. While the band played, the rooters used brooms to demonstrate "a clean sweep of Texas A&M." The cadets, already irritated by the score, which showed them behind, rushed the field and a brawl ensued. Texas student William Trenekmann came out of the fracas with stab wounds and was hospitalized. After peace was restored, the Longhorns finished cutting out a 24–8 win.

Attempts were made to patch things up before the Thanksgiving meeting. *The Texan* claimed that false reports of bad blood between the schools and "unjust criticism" had strained the relations. The Austin students made a gesture of good will by holding a welcoming parade for the cadets. With the Texas students in one line and the cadets and their band in another, the groups marched from the train depot to the Capitol. This is not to

After coach N. A. Merriam left under the cover of darkness, Charles Moran improved A&MC's football fortune by coaching the Farmers to an undefeated season in 1909.

The repertoire of the 'Varsity Band was altered when, in 1908, it was forced to omit a yell with the word hell *in it.*

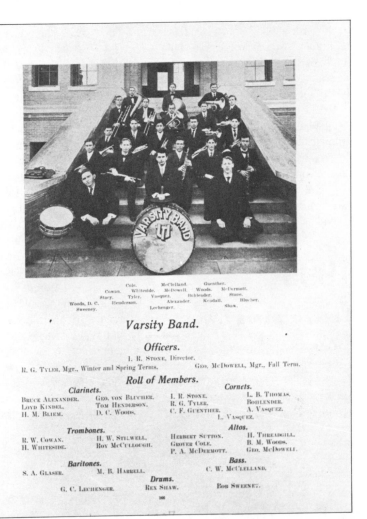

Cole.   McClelland.   Guenther.
Cowan.   Whiteside.   McDowell.   Woods.   McDermott.
Stacy.   Tyler.   Vasquez.   Bohlender.   Stone.
Woods, D. C.   Henderson.   Alexander.   Kendall.   Blucher.
Sweeney.   Lechenger.   Shaw.

Varsity Band.

Officers.

I. R. Stone, Director.

R. G. Tyler, Mgr., Winter and Spring Terms.   Geo. McDowell, Mgr., Fall Term.

Roll of Members.

Clarinets.
Bruce Alexander.   Geo. von Blucher.
Loyd Kindel.   Tom Henderson.
H. M. Bliem.   D. C. Woods,

Cornets.
I. R. Stone.   L. B. Thomas.
R. G. Tyler.   Bohlender.
C. F. Guenther.   A. Vasquez.
L. Vasquez.

Trombones.
R. W. Cowan.   H. W. Stilwell.
H. Whiteside.   Roy McCullough.

Altos.
Herbert Sutton.   H. Threadgill.
Grover Cole.   B. M. Woods.
P. A. McDermott.   Geo. McDowell.

Baritones.
S. A. Glaser.   M. B. Harrell.

Bass.
C. W. McClelland.

Drums.
G. C. Lechenger.   Rex Shaw.   Bob Sweeney.

166

While the UT band played loose and free, the Aggie Band marched to a different drummer.

say no fierce attitudes remained. *The Texan* put it thus: "We can lose to everybody else but that we must defeat A&M has long been the sentiment here, and it is the same way on the Farmers' side of the fence."

A&M fenced the Longhorns throughout the first half, and took a 12–0 lead on three drop-kicked field goals, one a fifty-yarder. Between halves (there was no "interhalf parade"), some Texas exes spoke to their boys and fired them up. Again and again they smashed into the Farmers' line through the second half, beating the visitors, 28–12.

1909

The Farmers Sweep

A&M's second-year coach N. A. Merriam instructed his team to a victory over Austin College in the 1909 opener. But when puny Texas Christian University tied them, 0–0, a clamor went up for his hide. By nightfall, sto-

ries have it, the student body had raised enough money to pay Merriam off, and he slipped out of town. Charles Moran was named successor. Moran was the school's eighth football coach; only one, J. E. Platt, had been able to pin a defeat on 'Varsity. Moran's tenure would fan the flames that had started burning a year earlier in the riot at Houston. He was controversial and successful during his stay at A&MC, and Texas officials didn't like him. He beat 'Varsity.

Football remained a violent sport, which Moran didn't mind. The player qualification rules remained somewhat elastic, which Moran didn't mind either. A player had to have been attending classes for one day prior to a game. Moran took liberal advantage of this opportunity. In the 1960s, Caesar "Dutch" Hohn, who played tackle for Moran in 1909–12, would tell Wilbur Evans (co-author with H. B. McElroy of the fine history of Texas A&M football, *The Twelfth Man*) that "four students of questionable athletic pedigree" left school immediately after the second Texas game of 1909. Hohn and end

Charles DeWare (1905–08) were named in 1969 to the All-Southwest team for the first half-century.

In the first game, played in a downpour at Houston's No-Tsu-Oh, Moran coached the second Farmer win in seventeen games with Texas, 23–0. A&M recovered a fumble early and scored, then quickly crossed Texas' goal again and 'Varsity never recovered.

The Thanksgiving matchup at Clark Field took on a different complexion, remaining scoreless until the second half. The Farmers stopped five Texas drives deep in A&M territory. Victor Kelley's touchdown put A&M ahead, then teammate Louis Hamilton followed by circling left end and scampering ninety yards for an apparent TD, but he was called back for stepping out of bounds upfield. The five points earned by Kelley's run were enough, however, and the Longhorns swallowed their second loss to A&M in a foundering 4–3–1 season. Moran's 7–0–1 was the best record in history at College Station. He would haunt 'Varsity again.

The A&M Athletic Council wanted to eliminate violence in football, which was giving the sport a bad name.

1910

Three in a Row

Thirty-two deaths across the United States fueled the fire over football violence. *The Houston Post* listed the damage in some detail:

Deaths 32	
College players	**9**
High school players	**20**
Athletics	**3**
Injuries 220	
Broken jaws	**3**
Fractured skulls	**4**
Broken noses	**8**
Paralysis	**2**
Broken legs	**15**
Broken arms	**9**
Broken collarbones	**13**
Brain concussions	**22**
Fractured ribs	**20**
Misc. (teeth, scalp wounds, cuts)	**52**

Forrest E. Craver of Dickinson College suggested some first aid; Craver wouldn't go down in history as a great football mind:

1. No player on the line of scrimmage may run back of his own scrimmage line after ball is put in play unless he be the player to receive a pass or to run with the ball.
2. No forward pass may go beyond the line of scrimmage.
3. Fair catch must be made of all kicks.

Craver had other plans of even less merit.

But Charles Moran merited a lot in the eyes of Texas A&M followers. He sculpted a ten-game winning streak by the middle of his second year. It would be the University of Arkansas that bombed Moran's Utopia, 5–0. But A&M remained a formidable gridiron machine when it faced Texas at Houston in the third year of A&M's contract with the No-Tsu-Oh festival officials. The college's authorities felt the school hadn't been treated properly in the number of seats set up and the quantity of tickets sent for sale in College Station. After all, a cadet had to pay $1 for a railroad ticket plus $1.50 to see the game, and he ought to be assured a good seat. A thousand cadets were among the 9,000–10,000 people crammed into West End Park's grandstand facilities, which were designed for 8,000.

They saw A&M kick a field goal, now worth three points, a minute and a half into the game. Then they saw Texas "seem to give up," according to *The Texan*. The Farmers triumphed for the third straight time, 14–8, then paddled the rest of their foes for an eight-win season, their most successful ever. William "Silent Billy" Wasmund's Texas club finished at 6–2, including a 1–0 forfeit victory over Baylor, whose members refused to compete after a disputed call.

The Battalion *staff gears up on deadline, 1908.*

Aggies stand ready to defend their alma mater.

In an effort to avoid the April Fool's Day pranks of mischievous cadets, officials organized the annual Hike to the Brazos. Once there, all manner of military maneuvers were practiced.

Cane Rush, an annual brawl between A&MC sophomores and juniors, leaves participants exhausted and ragged.

Women were scarce at College Station in 1900, but Aggie ingenuity prevailed and provided everyone a date for the Senior Dress Ball.

Aggies study the bare bones of anatomy.

The "country club" atmosphere of living quarters at Texas contrasted greatly with College Station's tent row.

Among members of the first A&MC team to defeat Texas was Josh Sterns (top row, fourth from right), the state's first football scout.

1910's

1911

UT Quits on Top

Billy Wasmund had spent three years quarterbacking for Michigan, and his reputation was that of a brainy field general. Now, at twenty-six, the likable Texas coach was expected to field a strong contender to end Texas A&M's string. But on the Saturday before the Longhorns' opener with TCU, Wasmund fell from the second floor of his home while sleepwalking, sustaining a blow to the head. Assistant coach William Disch took over drills after Wasmund was hospitalized.

Wasmund died on the Wednesday following his fall. The team from TCU consented to cancel their game as the state university went into mourning. Little time was wasted, however, in obtaining a new mentor. David W. Allerdice arrived October 9, his train running twelve hours late. A large welcoming crowd had dwindled to three people by the time he stepped to the depot platform. He immediately spoke kindly of his predecessor, who had been his teammate in 1907–09 at Mich-

William Disch took over Texas' coaching duties following Billy Wasmund's accident.

igan. It seems that Allerdice had beaten out Wasmund for the Wolverine captaincy in 1909 by two or three votes. "The first person to congratulate me," Allerdice said, "was Billy Wasmund."

Allerdice picked up the pieces and, before long, was 4–1 and facing A&M. The rivals to the east were unscored on in four games, which included notable defeats of Auburn and Mississippi. Charles Moran had never

lost to Texas, an unusual claim for an A&M coach. For that, and for what orange and white partisans considered his teams' bully tactics, he was immensely disliked in Austin. Both schools sent notes to the game officials instructing them to referee a football game, not a wrestling match. Rumors of eligibility problems worried alumni from both schools, but everybody played. Texas brought thirty-two players and A&M thirty-five to yet another state championship game in Houston.

Allerdice considered his Texas team as good as any he'd seen at Michigan. When Arnold Kirkpatrick scooped up an A&M fumble and fell into the end zone while being tackled, Texas won, 6–0, for what Disch described as "the sweetest victory ever over A&M." Jim Hart, captain of Texas' 1900 team, had tears in his eyes during the celebration after the game. Hundreds partied at the Thalian Club until 11:30, when they adjourned to catch their train to Austin.

The following day, the A&M athletic department received a letter stating that the athletic council at Texas had decided not to enter into athletic relations with A&M in 1912.

Dormitory conditions at A&M were improving by 1911.

William O. Murray was named to the All-Texas conference team as a center in 1913.

1912–1914

Time Out

Texas gave no reasons for cutting athletic ties. Theories abound.

Dutch Hohn figured Charles Moran was the problem: Texas wouldn't play A&M until Moran was replaced and in the process "all but sent the [A&M] athletic department into bankruptcy." The idea is more than plausible. Moran was so disliked at the university that a special cheer was directed at him:

> To hell, to hell with Charley Moran
> And all his dirty crew.
> If you don't like the words of this song,
> To hell, to hell with you.

Another A&M alumnus, James M. "Cop" Forsyth ('12), pinned the break to the Houston riot of 1908. "Texas wanted to break it off after the next year," Forsyth would surmise in 1980, "but they didn't want to end it on a loss. They had to play us three more years before they beat us." In addition, there were reports that another student brawl

"I didn't come here to lose." Charley Moran left A&M after his sixth season; some said it was because Texas refused to resume the Farmer series as long as Moran was coach.

TO THE MEMORY
OF
CHARLES B. MORAN
GREAT COACH
OF
THE TEXAS AGGIES
1909 – 1914

HIS INDOMITABLE SPIRIT AND INSPIRING LEADERSHIP ARE ENSHRINED FOREVER IN THE RECORDS OF THE TEAMS WHICH HE PRODUCED AND IN THE HEARTS OF THE AGGIES WHO PLAYED FOR HIM.

"I DIDN'T COME HERE TO LOSE"

A&M later erected a plaque in Moran's honor, 1949.

broke out after the 1911 game. Also, some orange-clad spectators swore they had seen an Aggie player grab the leg of a Texas player sticking out of a pileup and twist it until the bone broke. Another fan claimed he watched while a Texas ball carrier suffered a slug to the stomach from an A&M player while being tackled.

In any event, the two schools did not meet in athletic contests through 1914. Moran's 1912 squad won seven of eight games and his 1914 Farmers, six of eight. Despite his four-year mark of 38–8–4 (which remains today the best for an A&M coach), Charley Moran would coach no more at College Station. In December 1914 he either quit or the school refused to renew his contract. By 1919 he would be head coach at Centre College in Kentucky as his Praying Colonels headed for a dramatic meeting with Texas A&M.

The Texas Longhorns were also strong during the interim. They totaled twenty-two wins against two losses over the three seasons. The single loss in 1913 was 30–7 to Notre Dame, which played most of its games on the road to showcase its gridiron might around the country. That Austin encounter was the first of an eight-game Texas-Notre Dame series that would culminate in the heart-stopping Cotton Bowl clashes of the 1970s.

It was the formation of the Southwest Conference in 1914, sponsoring competition in football, basketball, baseball, and track and field, that brought the state's two old enemies together again.

1915

Winning for Love

"You won't win at College Station." That was A&M's message to Texas while Southwest Conference blueprints were being drafted. Under A&M's demand that the two establish a home-and-home football schedule, the first game would be at A&M.

SWC competition was christened in January with a Rice-Baylor basketball game in Houston. It would be Texas, however, behind the scoring of captain Clyde Littlefield, that would win the first league cage crown. Under Uncle Billy Disch's coaching, Texas won the initial baseball championship, and the first track and field title went to Austin, too, thanks again to help from Littlefield.

The only vacancy in the Longhorns' trophy case was where the football award might have gone. Baylor and Oklahoma tied for that, each with a 3–0 mark, but the Bears relinquished their grip when it was found an ineligible player had been used.

Despite A&M's warning to Texas, the meeting at College Station was congenial. The college's rooters sang "Auld Lang Syne" in honor of the resumption of relations. Both sets of cheerleaders courteously led the opposing supporters in cheers, and at halftime nearly 1,000 Longhorn rooters paraded in front of the cadets' stands and cheered the Farmers before beginning their own yells. When the cadets took the field, they formed a "T" for the Texas fans.

Still, Charley Moran had a hand in the proceedings. He had written every A&M player from his home in Kentucky and urged them to "Beat those people from Austin. If

A&M's 1915 team displays the score that would later be branded on the minds of all Texas players. Team captain J. P. Garrity holds the ball.

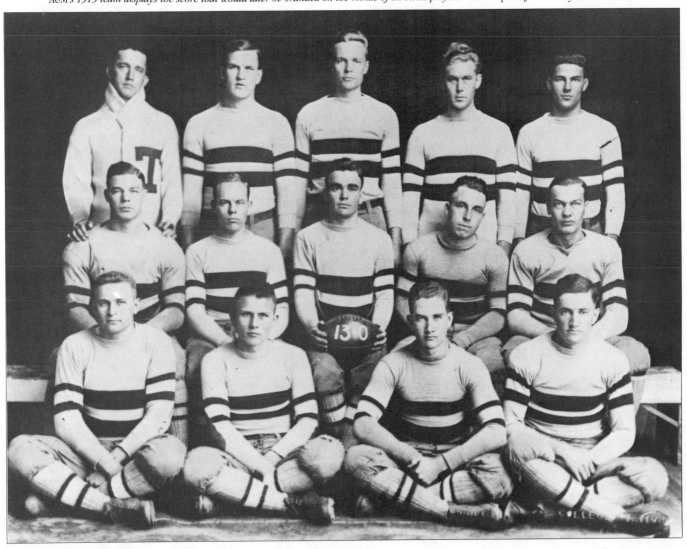

"You won't win at College Station." An Aggie ball-carrier makes a move against Texas as the Farmers establish the Kyle Field jinx during the first year of Southwest Conference play, 1915.

you still love me and think anything of me, then beat Texas." Leaders of the A&M teams Texas had refused to play since 1911 were on hand to lend support.

Under the guidance of Moran's replacement, E. H. Harlan from the University of Pittsburgh, the Farmers proved that the "You won't win" warning had been accurate. Texas gained double the yardage of A&M and made nine first downs to the Farmers' three. But the home team's defense was brilliant, causing twelve Texas fumbles. A&M scored after two of them and notched a 13–0 conference victory. Littlefield, who had stacked up eleven touchdowns during the year, couldn't break the A&M defense.

The cadets carried their heroes from the field, then helped Texas' rooters carry their players to the dressing room. The rivalry was mended.

The Bryan Eagle summed it up: "A&M stands head and shoulders above all others as State champion world without end."

1916

"Thanks for Beating Us"

By Thanksgiving, the folks up Bryan way were still basking in the glow of the previous year's victory. A&M's annual, named *The Longhorn* before Texas' athletic teams were, looked back on the 13–0 triumph as "one experience, one day that stands out vividly above all other experiences."

People at the university took it no less seriously. On Monday, November 21, a pep rally was held to boost spirit. That there was a league game with Southwestern before the A&M game nine days hence was of little importance. Southwestern was hardly mentioned. The collective mind of the University of Texas dwelled solely on Texas A&M.

Southwestern, which didn't win an SWC

game before dropping out of the league after the 1916 season, did indeed fall to the Longhorns, 17–3. Among victims in Texas' six wins (in eight games) had been Southern Methodist University (74–0) and league foe Arkansas (52–0). The Farmers' effort had added up to an identical 6–2 mark, including a 62–0 defeat of SMU and a 77–0 hammering of the Missouri School of Mines.

Hundreds of Texas alumni were among the 15,000 who attended the A&M game, the first at Clark Field since 1909. W. A. Rhea, an 1894 Texas graduate, told his friends before the game, "I saw the first real team 'Varsity ever had and helped to make it go, not by playing but by rooting. I can't miss this one."

Only the Farmers wished they had. Texas deflated A&M, 21–7, on sweeping end runs and dazzling fake plays. William Lang scampered forty yards for a touchdown. The celebration was such that Texas' president, R. E. Vinson, declared the following Friday a school holiday.

A&M demonstrates the forward pass in a game against Baylor, 1916. First approved under a 1906 change of rules, the pass didn't result in any touchdowns in this 3–0 Farmer victory.

A&M's president, W. B. Bizzell, had a singular view of the loss. In a speech to the postgame crowd, Bizzell thanked the university and the city of Austin for a pleasant visit. "It would have been rank ingratitude for our team to have beaten them on this afternoon. It was a great day for both institutions and I'm glad that nothing occurred to mar the pleasure of the perfect day."

No team was named Southwest Conference champion because every school had lost a game. Texas finished atop the heap, however, at 5–1.

1917

The Birth of Bevo

Three years before Texas A&M lined up its first football team, a child had been born in Tennessee who would come to have a profound effect on A&M and its premier competitor, Texas. Dana Xenophon Bible grew up to be a Latin scholar while attending Brandon Prep School in Shelbyville, Tennessee. But he preferred to examine the teachings of

the great football minds of the day. Bible got his first taste of coaching at Brandon. When he advanced to the coaching position at Mississippi, he took a youngster from Brandon with him, named Frank G. Anderson, who would make waves of his own far away in College Station, Texas.

In 1916, Bible became Texas A&M's freshman football coach, under E. H. Harlan. At mid-season, Louisiana State ran off its head coach and requested the services of Dana Bible for the rest of the season. A&M officials agreed and Bible coached LSU's final three games—a win over Ole Miss and ties with Rice and Tulane. LSU was so pleased that it wanted to keep the balding young Tennessean. But Bible went back. "I felt a moral obligation to A&M," he would recount later. "I was delighted and honored to return as head coach."

The school was glad to have him back. A&M played eight foes in his first year as head coach and not one of them scored a point. Landslide victims included Austin College (66–0) and Dallas University (98–0).

Students at Texas planned to bring a live longhorn steer, branded with the 21–7 score

of 1916's game, to the Thanksgiving Day battle in 1917. But after the plans became known in College Station, three cadets found their way into the steer's stall in Austin the week before the game and branded him with 13–0, the result of that fine 1915 fight. The animal's handlers, upon finding the brand, altered the characters to resemble the letters *BEVO*. Thus was christened, if somewhat excessively, Bevo I. The beast made its social debut at the A&M game, as scheduled, but even then he didn't look too good. He was served as steak at an A&M-Texas get-together in 1921, and his head was mounted on a wall of Texas' athletic offices.

The 1917 football game was scoreless late in the second half. When A&M missed a field goal attempt, the sky looked dark for the Farmers and their unbeaten record. But a Texas player was offside and A&M was granted a first down. On fourth down, Danny McMurrey, a 200-pound tackle playing offensive back, scored the winning touchdown. A&M had won the second College Station war with Texas, 7–0. The Farmers downed Rice a week later for its fourth undefeated season and first SWC title.

"Aeroplane View" of College Station, 1917.

Dana Bible (front row, right) *coached a team that boasted three All-Southwest Conference players: Rip Collins* (fourth row, fifth from left), *Ox Ford* (top row, second from left), *and Tim Greisenbeck* (top row, sixth from left).

Cadets pose with their prisoner, the Rice Owl, stolen shortly before the branding of Bevo, 1917.

1918

Making Do

Not many battles were considered more important than the Texas-A&M football game, but the war in Europe, of course, was one. Both teams were decimated by the call to service, and Dana X. Bible spent 1918 as a pur-

suit pilot. The year was almost a quiet interlude in the schools' tumultuous relationship.

The Southwest Conference continued its youthful metamorphosis. Of the charter members besides A&M and Texas, there remained Oklahoma, Arkansas, Baylor, and Oklahoma A&M. Rice had taken leave after 1915 but was participating again by 1918. Outmanned Southwestern had withdrawn permanently, and its coach J. Burton Rix ob-

tained the same job at SMU in time for that school's SWC inauguration in 1918. Coach Bill Juneau's Longhorns chalked up Texas' fifth undefeated season—including a 32–0 rout of the Mustangs—and for the second time landed atop the conference statistics in a year in which no champion was named. Its schedule was a weak one, however, including Radio School (twice), Ream Flying Field, and Auto Mechanics School. A&M's

The branding bunch prepares for its meeting with Bevo.

34

slate read similarly, though. Ream Field, Camp Travis, Camp Mabry, and Camp Travis Remount Station helped the Farmers carve their 6–1 record under coach D. V. Graves. Rosters were so thin throughout the conference that no All-SWC team was selected.

When the two teams met in Austin before a crowd of 7,500—half the number who saw the 21–7 revenge action two years before—both were undefeated. Their statistics read like those in so many other years: Texas and A&M had scored and scored while their opponents had tallied fourteen and twelve points, respectively. Still, the two teams, skeletal images of their former powerful selves, battled fiercely following first quarter touchdown run by Longhorn Joe Ellis. In the last quarter, the determined Farmers moved the ball the length of the field only to be stopped short and forced to suffer a 7–0 setback.

H. H. Rothe (left), *red hot iron in hand, warms up for a little cattle branding, 1917.*

No longer willing to feed their dishonored mascot, some Texas students suggest the $18-a-day cost of his upkeep should become A&M's. They suggest the beast be sent to College Station C.O.D.

Texas coaching staff, 1919 (from left to right): *Berry Whitaker, H. J. Ettlinger, Eugene Van Gent, and Bill Juneau.*

1919

The Real Stuff

Dana Bible returned from Europe to lead the Texas A&M football team in an autumn of strafing defenseless opponents. Through his second year as coach, his teams never took a hit, as Bible deployed the Aggies' relentless defense. Sam Houston State Teachers College fell, 28–0. Then came SMU, Howard Payne, Trinity, and the SWC enemies. Howard Payne kept them close (12–0); so did Baylor (10–0) and Southwestern (7–0). But the key to each game was the A&M defense. Going into the Texas game, no team had ever scored against a Bible-coached Farmer squad.

Despite such evidence of power on the A&M side, the smartest bettors weren't putting too much on the table. They had learned in the early years that the A&M-Texas squabble was different from football at any other time or place. The *Austin American* saw fit to note that "both teams always enter the Turkey Day game as equal favorites." Though the *American* staff apparently felt pressed to predict the score of the following day's game, it would not commit itself: "The Lord only knows."

Texas would try to bring down Bible's victory machine with an offense that had scored

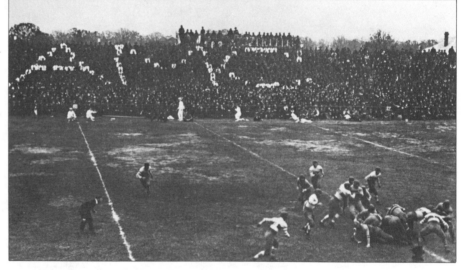

A&M's Jack Mahan, All-Southwest Conference fullback, breaks through the Longhorn line for a gain at Kyle Field, 1919.

181 points while shooting down six of eight opponents. A&M had scored 268.

The Farmers added seven more points to their point total in the College Station clash; Texas added none to theirs. Employing what was known as "straight football," Bible's boys staked themselves to a touchdown lead in the second quarter, then put everything they had into their vaunted defense. The result was Bible's second unscored-upon season. The nation's football enthusiasts were beginning to notice Texas A&M.

It was after World War I that J. V. "Pinky" Wilson, former A&M student, wrote the Texas A&M War Hymn while standing guard on the Rhine. Introduced in 1921, the Hymn was to taunt old 'Varsity for decades:

Good-bye to Texas University.
So long to the Orange and the White.
Good luck to the dear old Texas Aggies,
They are the boys who show the fight.
The eyes of Texas are upon you,
This is the song they sing so well,
So, goodbye to Texas University,
We're going to beat you all to—
Chig-gar-roo-gar-rem!
Chig-gar-roo-gar-rem!
Rough! Tough!
Real stuff! Texas A&M!

1920

The "Greatest Ever"

"When I came to Texas A&M from Mississippi College to coach the freshman football team," Frank G. Anderson would recall in 1980, "it was a rough place. The freshmen had to go through nine months of hazing and a lot of them couldn't take it. They'd go home at Christmas and not come back. Rough! Tough! Real stuff! Texas A&M! We thought of the boys at Texas as teasippers."

When Bible's third Farmer football team trampled Daniel Baker College 110–0 in the season opener, notice was given that life in the Southwest Conference would indeed be rough and tough. SMU lost by only a field goal, however, and LSU got even, literally, with their one-time head coach by tying A&M 0–0. Opponents' number one objective was to score against the Aggies' invulnerable defense. Opponent number six, Baylor, came close. The Aggies held the Bears four downs at the A&M one-yard line. Later, Baylor employed a hidden-ball trick in its own end of the field. The Aggie defenders finally figured out who had the ball and pulled him down at the one. A&M held and remained unscored on a 24–0 finish. Rice fell to A&M the next week, 7–0, before the time came to give Texas a shot at the streak. By now, the Aggie goal was uncrossed by the twenty-five opponents Bible's teams had faced.

The game with the Longhorns was in Austin, though, and the Aggies hadn't done well there. "The greatest athletic contest ever played in Texas," as the *Austin American* dubbed it, was fought before the largest crowd, 20,000. "The A&M game is at hand," announced *The Texan*, "and classes and quizzes are mere details."

Coach Berry Whitaker's first team was possibly the best Texas squad ever. None of its previous eight foes had gotten to within seventeen points of the Longhorns; only two had even scored. The Thanksgiving Day classic exhibited the immovable object versus the irresistible force.

The Aggies erected a 3–0 lead as per plan and held on. Texas' Whitaker alternated Kyle "Icky" Elam and Grady "Rat" Watson at quarterback. Their five passes plus an effective running game ate up over 200 yards, but A&M's heralded defense held again and again. In the fourth quarter, Texas used a shift to make tackle Tom Dennis eligible, and he caught a Bill Barry pass at the Aggies' three-yard line. On the next play, Francis J. Domingues blemished Dana Bible's unmarked career at A&M and handed Texas its first Southwest Conference championship. The 7–3 bout remains one of the most celebrated in the annals of A&M-Texas warfare.

A&M scores a field goal against the 'Horns, 1920.

A&M President William Bizzell enjoys the 1920 game.

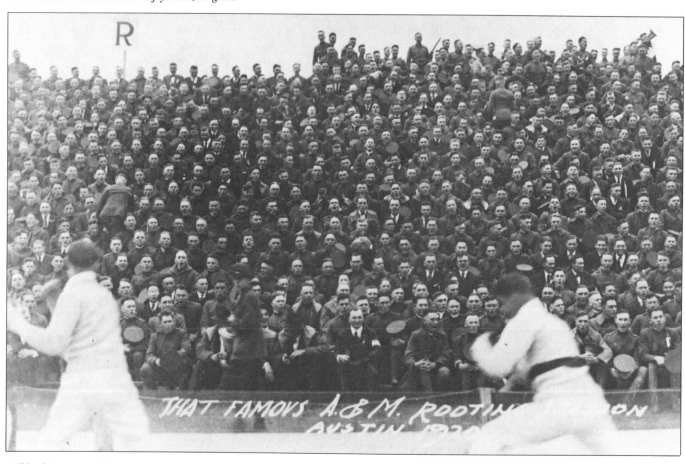

Yell leaders spur on A&M rooting section, 1920.

Dana Bible arrived at A&M in 1917; his teams went unscored upon for his first twenty-five games.

"Goodbye to Texas University." A&M band forms the Aggie T, *1920.*

During halftime at the 1921 game, Texas Cowboys tout the score of the historic 1920 UT-A&M battle.

Cadets overload a handcar at College Station, 100 miles from Austin.

Seniors who failed to receive officer commissions took the name of Veterans of the Lost Cause and, dressed appropriately, posed for their group picture.

1920's

1921

The Twelfth Man Appears

"Hardly had the play been completed until the world outside knew what had happened." The 1921 A&M-Texas encounter, in which the Aggies overcame seven fumbles to preserve a 0–0 tie and its Kyle Field jinx over the 'Horns, was the first football game reported by wireless. Progress of the game was known in Austin and across the nation within minutes.

Dressing room oratory reached its peak nationwide during the '20s and '30s, and Texas had been the victim of one of the more stirring pre-game entreaties. Before their game in Dallas, Vanderbilt's players heard their legendary coach, Earle McGugin, softly ask them, "Who the devil started all this bunk about the Texas team? Who thinks they are unbeatable? They say they have the greatest team in history. They say that Vanderbilt never had a team which could beat theirs this year, but that is not true." McGugin exhorted each player to "fight every inch of the way" and not "live in contempt of his teammates for the rest of his days." A fired up Vandy team handed the Longhorns their only 1921 loss, 20–0.

For the Aggies, the season began their favorite tradition and produced a victory that remains one of the school's greatest. After the 0–0 tie with Texas, the Southwest Conference champion Farmers were invited to bring their 5–1–2 record to the Dixie Classic, forerunner of the Cotton Bowl, on January 2, 1922. Their opponents were the Praying Colonels of Centre College, coached by former Aggie leader Charley Moran. The Colonels were the glamour team of football, having upset Harvard 6–0 in an undefeated year. They were twenty-point favorites against A&M; the *Dallas Journal* gave odds against the Farmers at 4–1. But Coach Bible told his players that many of Centre's stars were just Texans like themselves. Quarterback Alvin "Bo" McMillin and lineman Matty Bell, among other Centre players, were from Fort Worth, and there were a few Dallasites on the roster, too.

T. F. "Puny" Wilson, the Aggie end who made All-SWC three years, later described the pre-game scene at Dallas' Fair Park: "Mr.

King Gill, the original Twelfth Man, 1922.

Lettermen at A&M were proud wearers of the Aggie T, 1920–21.

Bible spoke a few well-chosen words and man, we were ready!" Referee Ernie Quigley would recall, "I've never seen a team as ready to play as A&M." Sammy Sanders, who also grabbed All-SWC honors that year at running back, was so nervous he fumbled the opening kickoff but picked it up and sped forty-five yards through the Centre team. The Aggies eventually scored first, with a safety, then Centre went ahead on a touchdown. But the Colonels proceeded to fumble twice, and A&M scored after each.

It was a hard-hitting affair. As injuries cut into the Aggies' reserves, Bible called for King Gill, a sophomore working in the press box, to come down and put on a suit. He never got into the game, but was ready if needed. To this day, the Aggie Cadet Corps stands throughout the game, symbolic of the Twelfth Man, King Gill, ready if needed.

A&M won 22–14 over its controversial ex-mentor and his glamour boys. Moran, whose 122–33–12 (.766) record at A&M, Centre, Bucknell, and Catawba would make

him one of the game's most successful coaches ever, said, "The Aggies displayed the old fighting spirit, and I am free to state that I had rather be whipped by them than any other eleven." Tiny Maxwell of the *Philadelphia Evening Public Ledger* wrote that "the A&M team played unbeatable football . . . one of the greatest football teams ever assembled." Referee Quigley believed that "the Aggies' victory stamped the brand of football played in the Southwest as equal to that offered anywhere."

1922

Crossing the Line

At halftime of the 1922 Texas game, Dana Bible called on history most successfully. The teams were tied 7–7 at Clark Field, where A&M had never won an SWC game.

Bible remembered that, in a story now discredited by most historians, Colonel

William Travis drew a line on the dirt floor of the Alamo and invited all who wanted to stay and fight the huge Mexican force to step over the line. They all stepped over, according to the legend, except Jim Bowie, who was seriously wounded and had to be carried over on his cot. In Clark Field's visitors' locker room, Bible drew an imaginary line across the floor with his shoe and told his players, "Those who want to go out and be known as the first members of an A&M team that defeated Texas in Austin, step over the line." Bible dodged the ensuing rush, and A&M won, 14–7.

Such a brazen tactic was typical of Bible. Joel Hunt, all-conference halfback at A&M from 1925–1927, would describe his coach as "confident as a banker, astute as a schoolmaster, poised as a preacher and expressive as a salesman." Bible won five Southwest Conference titles at A&M, six Big 6 championships at Nebraska (where he coached from 1929–1936), and three more at Texas (1937–1946), for an astounding total of

Star quarterback Alvin "Bo" McMillin was married on the field before the Dixie Classic, January 2, 1922.

Arno "Shorty" Nowotny exhibits the winning form of a Texas yell leader, 1922.

takes a leading part in the activities. The mention of A&M at any time will bring a surly growl from him. If the words are repeated, he is apt to go into a tantrum and tear whatever he seizes first." ●

1923

Bluestein's Revenge

With Ed Bluestein as captain, the 1923 Longhorns dealt death blows to their first six opponents, none of whom scored. Texas was tied 7–7 by Baylor, but then beat Oklahoma. The Baylor game hardly mattered. The Steers, most particularly "Blue," had their eyes on Thanksgiving Day. Bluestein talked about beating the Aggies all year.

Despite their undefeated record, the 'Horns weren't expected to defeat A&M. In four games against the Aggies at College Station, Texas had never scored. The sight of orange jerseys on their territory lifted Aggies to an emotional high in every odd year. All seats were, of course, grabbed up days in advance.

fourteen major conference titles in twenty-nine seasons with three different teams. That got him into the National Football Coaches Hall of Fame in 1951, as soon as he was eligible five hears after he quit coaching. His mark at five colleges was 192–71–23 (.712). Every honor in football was bestowed upon the man.

After A&M's Austin win in 1922 the Texas locker room was a dismal place. Players sat around moaning and groaning about their performance. A senior named Ed Bluestein stood up and hollered, "I'll tell you what I'm going to do about it. Tomorrow I'm calling my calculus prof and having him flunk me so I can come back next year and get another crack at those Aggies!" And that's just what he did.

There was somebody else around the Austin campus who didn't like what he'd heard about Texas A&M. His name was Pig Bellmont, and he was an orange and white spotted bulldog mascot (named for UT Athletic Director L. Theo Bellmont). *The Texan* reported, "Pig is old now, little to say. Only time he ever really comes out of his shell is at the annual game between the university and Texas A&M. Pig suddenly comes to life and

Texas Cowboys add a footnote to history, 1922.

During practice on the Monday before Thanksgiving, Ed Bluestein broke his leg. The pain, he said later, was not in his ankle but in the fact that he wouldn't get to play in the A&M game. He made sure he was on the sideline in a cast, however, and before the game he grabbed his replacement and said, "Kid, if you don't play the best damn game of your life, I'll kill you." Enough Longhorns played their "best damn game" to defeat A&M on a fumble recovery that led to a first-quarter touchdown. It was the only tally in Texas' 6–0 "miracle victory."

As for Ed Bluestein, he spent a few years as a coaching assistant at Texas, and then joined the Texas Department of Public Safety—whereupon he was assigned to the Bryan office. "Blue" came to appreciate Aggie football, but Texas would always remain his favorite.

Walter S. Hunnicutt and Burnett Pharr produced their "Texas Taps," later to be known as "Texas Fight," in 1923. The lyrics included a Longhorn counterpunch: "Texas fight! Texas fight! And it's goodbye to A&M."

Ed Bluestein, captain of the 1923 Longhorns, wanted one more crack at the Aggies.

"The mention of A&M at any time will bring a growl from him." Pig Bellmont is honored after his death with a funeral procession down the Drag, 1923.

1924

The Original Immaculate Reception

"Today is the greatest of all days for everyone ever so remotely connected at any time with the University of Texas or Texas A&M College," blared the *Austin American* on the morning of Thanksgiving Day.

The Longhorns' victory at Kyle Field in 1923 had spurred Texas students and alumni to contribute generously to a stadium fund, and the first concrete stadium in the south was erected in Austin. More seating for the A&M game was the new structure's primary purpose, and Memorial Stadium was dedicated at the Thanksgiving battle.

More than 35,000 crammed into the new bowl, including UT Coach "Doc" Stewart's mother, who had come from Cleveland, Ohio, and three Texas governors—one past, one present, and one future. Twenty-one special trains carted two-thirds of that crowd into the capital, and street cars ran from the two depots to campus at two-minute intervals.

The punting of Fred Thompson and Stud Wright kept the visitors deep in their own territory, except for an Aggie drive that fizzled at Texas' two-yard line. The Aggie defense held, however, for more than three and a half quarters. With only five minutes remaining, Texas threw a fourth-down pass that soared way over the head of Stookie Allen, the intended receiver. The Aggie defender got his hands on it but, since it was fourth down, he batted it down rather than intercept it. The ball dropped into Allen's arms and the 'Horn receiver scored a touchdown.

Even before the crowd dispersed after Texas' 7–0 win, extra editions of *The Texan* were being distributed at the stadium, detailing the bizarre happenings. Some Aggie alumni were so disgruntled that they wanted Dana Bible fired immediately for the ricochet Texas touchdown.

Bob Berry evades Owl defenders in a 13–6 Farmer victory over Rice, 1924. No one knows what the fellow at the right is doing.

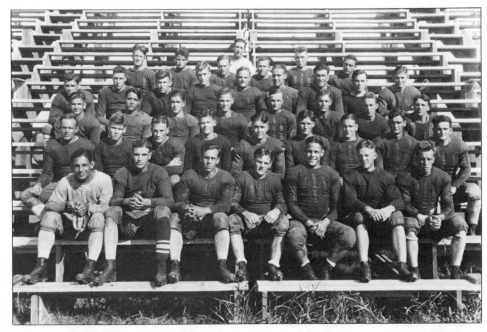

E. J. "Doc" Stewart (in white, rear center) *led the 1924 Longhorns to a 7–0 victory over the Aggies in the game's fading moments.*

The University of Texas' first student body, the class of 1884, returns to campus for a reunion, 1924.

Members of the UT class of 1924 whose parents had attended the University.

The Fightin' Texas Aggie Band leads the cadet corps to a game, 1925.

1925

"Wildcats"???

Curious goings-on enlivened 1920s football in the Lone Star State. SMU's star, Chris Cortemeglia, reportedly said he would walk back to Dallas if Texas beat the Mustangs in one Austin encounter. (The Austin press couldn't get a pre-game commitment from Cortemeglia concerning such a stroll, but the game's final score saved his feet anyway.)

The Daily Texan stationed a reporter in a hiding place where he could watch Texas Athletic Director Theo Bellmont move loads of wood back and forth between his shed and the street. The paper reported that the "mystery" had been solved—moving wood was Bellmont's way of exercising.

The university was realizing that oil on its 2 million acres in West Texas, endowed to it years earlier, would make it "the richest school in the world," in the words of *The Texan*. A&M, as a branch of the state university system, eventually would receive about one-third of the royalties, but there were constant "discussions" in regents' meetings and legislative groups over what the fair amount should be.

The Texan, opaquely insisting that "Wildcats" was the "official name" of the Aggies,

Theo Bellmont's athletic physique was partially the result of his lumber-hauling habit.

In 1925, the Aggies made an ass of Baylor and a goat of Rice.

provoked the motto, "The Horn is mightier than the claw." But Texas' Mack Saxon fumbled the opening kickoff, the Farmers smothered it and the 'Horns, 28–0. One Aggie touchdown came in the form of a ninety-two–yard interception return; another was scored on a fumble. Favored Texas had never suffered a league defeat so large, and the Aggies won their fourth SWC crown over second-place Texas.

1926

Fired Up

By the mid-1920s, the pre-game bonfire was a well-attended affair at both schools. At Texas, a pep rally usually accompanied the fete, and the coach and past players would give speeches predicting the fate of the unfortunate Aggies on Thanksgiving Day.

Sometimes these festivals caused problems. After Frank Anderson became A&M commandant in the mid-1930s, for example, he was confronted by an irate farmer who got up one day to discover his barn missing. "I found it, in parts, on the bonfire," Anderson recalled. A Texas fraternity once had to return 340 vegetable crates taken from an Austin market. Telephone and electric poles often were confiscated; outhouses, if discovered in time, were returned.

Tom Brown of the *Battalion* staff would later write:

One of the most indelible traditions of the Aggies is their bonfire each year before their march on Texas U. in football. Just at the approach of dusk, a two-story heap of lumber, collected by freshmen weeks in advance, is touched off. As its flames lick upward into the gathering gloom, cadets group around it to attend the elaborate "bull session" concerning the coming football battle with our ancient rival. During it is bared the Aggies' hopes, fears and dreams about football. The coach is there to tell us all our chances—to reassure us that our army will march however badly whipped, that although it has been torn and its personnel sore in body, every heart will fight until the final pistol, no muscle shall be idle for lack of spirit to command it. . . .

Several ex-students are there to recapture a moment or two of a carefree, happy past—maybe a few throats grow lumpy when "Farmers Fight" rolls up to heaven but there is no shame. . . . To an Aggie it means something that cannot be felt by an outsider—something that only an Aggie can feel!

In 1926, Aggie bonfires notwithstanding, a crowd of 40,000 (when Austin's population was less than 50,000) saw the 'Horns dismantle the Aggies, 14–5, in Doc Stewart's last game as coach.

1927

The Backward Pass

"He ain't so fast but you couldn't catch him in a telephone booth." That's how a contemporary described Texas A&M's brilliant quarterback, Joel Hunt (All-Southwest Conference in 1925, 1926, and 1927). The Farmers won the 1927 SWC crown by beating SMU in College Station as Hunt scored three touchdowns and passed for two more in the

The 1926 game gets under way before a crowd of 40,000 in Memorial Stadium.

Clyde Littlefield became UT's first All-Southwest Conference player in 1915. As Longhorn coach in 1927, he introduced the five-man line defense.

Dana Bible left A&M after the 1928 season to coach at Nebraska, a job Knute Rockne recommended him for.

sideline. "I'll never forget what Mr. Bible said to me when I came off the field," Burgess said. "He asked me why I stopped running and I said, 'Coach, I thought I'd scored.' He screamed, 'Burgess, you do all right until you start thinking, then you blow it completely!'"

The action was in the new version of Kyle Field, which was sold out. Clyde Littlefield, Texas' first All-SWC representative back in 1915, was the Longhorn coach, having replaced the sacked Doc Stewart. The 45,000 spectators produced an $80,000 gate, uncommon in those days. Texas fans vowed to bring down the new goal posts after a Longhorn victory, but the Aggies sent 'Horn fans away with a 28–7 loss instead.

1928

Bible's Good-Bye

Herschel Burgess would become an astute businessman, playing a major role in developing College Station into a thriving city. But during the 1928 football season he suffered through another inglorious moment in the game with Texas. He tells it best:

"The rules in those days provided that the play wasn't over until the referee's whistle blew," Burgess remembered. "You could roll around on the ground with the ball but the

39–13 win.

National sports columnist Billy Evans conjectured that Hunt missed making All-America only because the Farmers lacked national recognition. "I am convinced," Evans wrote, "that if Joel Hunt played in the Yale-Princeton game . . . he would be one of the most talked-about athletes in the sports world."

It was a Hunt pass to Jules Sikes against Texas that began one of the most talked-about plays in Aggie football history. Herschel E. Burgess, A&M fullback from 1926 to 1928, was unable to hide behind his laugh while describing the happenings fifty-three years after they occurred.

"Two games that stand out in my career," Burgess said in the office of his savings and loan firm in College Station, "were in '27. One was SMU, because we beat them after they'd beaten a Missouri team that had upset Harvard—that really shocked them in the East. The other game was Texas. We got a scouting report that Texas had changed its pass defense to man-to-man for our game. We worked hard on one play to counter that—the backward pass. Hunt threw over the middle to Sikes. I had delayed about two counts, then ran right by Sikes, who passed the ball back to me right after he caught it. I took off like a scalded dog."

But Burgess didn't score, despite having clear sailing to the goal. "I've got an alibi," he said. "That year the goalposts had been moved back to five yards behind the goal and I got mixed up. I slowed down when I passed the 10. A Texas boy hit me and I could have dragged him across the goal but I just flopped. I thought I'd scored!"

The Aggies got a touchdown on the drive, so nothing was lost. But Burgess' coach was anything but docile when they met on the

Rufus King, captain of the 1928 team, led the Longhorns to their second Southwest Conference title.

play wasn't over until that whistle blew. Well, I ran back a punt about 20 yards and was tackled. I got up and handed the ball to the referee but a Texas player ran between us and grabbed the ball, and the referee gave Texas possession, just because he hadn't blown his whistle yet."

It was Dana Bible's last game at A&M. The next year he would be at Nebraska, but his return to the Lone Star State in 1937 would again add spark to the Aggie-Longhorn rivalry.

Burgess recalled that the A&M-Texas series wasn't all spite. "Oh, the rivalry was natural, both being state schools and all, but it was a friendly one," he said. "I ran track and when we'd run in, say, the Kansas Relays and we'd see some Texas boys we'd always meet, introduce ourselves and wish each other luck." The track coach in Burgess' day was Frank Anderson, formerly Bible's assistant on the gridiron; Clyde Littlefield would resign as Texas' football coach in 1933, but he stayed on as track coach in Austin. His and Anderson's track squads kept the Southwest Conference title chase a two-man race.

In the 1928 football game in Austin, the Aggies were underdogs, so they tried some razzle-dazzle in the form of a hidden-ball play. The pigskin was placed in the flexed leg of an Aggie guard, but Texas end Bill Ford spotted it and grabbed it before the intended Aggie could. Ford lit out for the Aggie goal and Field Scovell, A&M's other guard, took off after him. Scovell caught Ford short of the goal line, but the Longhorns still had a 19–0 victory.

1929

Breaking a Leg for Old UT

The year had a wild beginning. There had been at least one off-the-bench tackle before 1929, and once two West Coast teams showed up to play a game but nobody had brought a ball. But nothing had ever equaled a play in the 1929 Rose Bowl for pure zaniness. California center Roy Riegels scooped up a Georgia Tech fumble in the game, became disoriented while avoiding would-be tacklers, and scampered sixty yards toward his own goal.

Tech players on the sideline jumped up in excitement but their coach was probably the calmest man in the stadium. "Sit down, sit down," Bill Alexander ordered his players. "He's just running the wrong way." Riegels' teammate Benny Lom chased him and stopped him at the California one-yard line. On the next play, Lom tried to punt out of trouble but the kick was blocked, giving Tech a safety, eventually enough to win the game, 8–7. After the play that would become the most famous in football history, Riegels played the entire second half and returned the next year to be elected team captain.

Things seemed to be going the wrong way as well ten months later in Austin. The University of Texas suspended sales of apples at its home games because most of the cores were sent flying toward the home team. Clyde Littlefield's squad was not the apple of the eyes of Texas with a 2–2–2 league mark (5–2–2 overall). One of those games was with Oklahoma at Dallas' Fair Park, marking resumption of that series and the beginning of Texas' other big rivalry.

In College Station, Madison Bell—the former Centre College star from Fort Worth—was trying to pump some life into the Aggie football program. It was in Bell's first year that A&M began giving athletic scholarships. Charley Cummings earned $25 a month for cleaning out DeWare Fieldhouse, but he didn't pass his schoolwork and left school. He wasn't around when Texas came to Kyle Field on Thanksgiving. In the thirty-fifth renewal of the rivalry, UT guard Curtis Beatty suffered a broken leg on the opening kickoff, forcing the Longhorns to alter their defense; thus adjusted, it stopped three A&M drives inside the Texas five-yard line. The Aggies, however, pushed the ball across the goal late in the third period and then went on to a 13–0 victory.

1930

Spirit, Determination, and Defeat

The social scene after the Texas-A&M game consisted of the annual dance. *The Texan*'s society page typically reported prior to a game in Austin that "no matter who wins the football game, the girls will be thrilled to dance with university students and maybe Aggies. Some of the girls are going so far as to have a date with an Aggie." But having a date didn't usually lift the gloom of an Aggie after an Austin game. A common moan at the dance was, "We would have done better but the jinx got us."

It wasn't so much the Austin jinx as Ernie Koy that got the Aggies, and the rest of the SWC, in 1930. Koy, whose sons would shine in the backfield for Darrell Royal, was star of the excellent Longhorn teams from 1930 to 1932. In 1930, Texas, with six All-SWC selections including Koy on its roster, beat the Aggies 26–0 en route to the conference championship. While Texas' only loss of the season was a 6–0 shocker to Rice, A&M Coach Matty Bell was already in the dog house, where his team finished in last place at 0–5.

The name "Wildcats" for A&M's athletic teams remained popular in Austin. After a *Texan* headline referred to Baylor's victory over the "Wildcats," the *Battalion*'s sports editor took exception, writing in a column that no animal in the world could accurately represent the spirit and determination of the Fightin' Texas Aggies, and that when such a word was chosen it would be done so by Texas A&M, not by a headline writer in Austin.

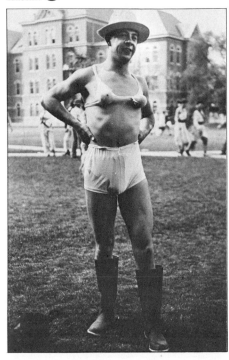

Though it often took a lot to cheer up a cadet following the annual clash with UT, the women who attended the post-game dance looked much better than the dancing partners found on the A&M campus.

The second expansion of Kyle Field in 1929 cost A&M $259,693.68, a debt retired eleven years later by Homer Norton, coach and head of the physical education department.

"Beware of our Wildcat."
Texas students escort the
Aggie "mascot" onto the field.

Crowds head for Kyle Field to witness
UT's triumph over the jinx, 1923.

Texas Cowboys form the Texas T, 1922.

Texas Cowboys and mascot, 1923.

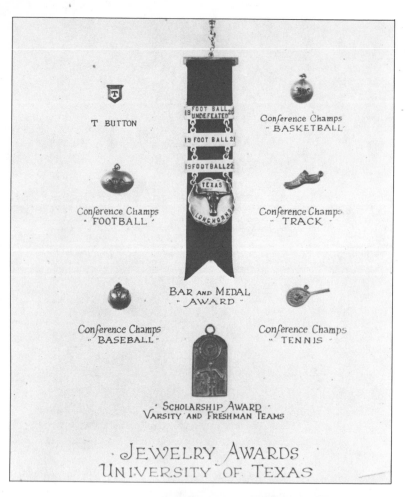

UT Jewelry Awards, 1922.

Students and alumni launched an intensive fund-raising campaign to build a stadium commemorating the Texas men and women who served in World War I. The students alone raised $150,000 in one week.

While the men at UT played football and other sports, university women refined their own athletic abilities through more "feminine" pursuits.

1930's

1931

And, Now, Reveille!

When a carload of cadets picked up a scared puppy on the highway near Navasota, it began a chapter of Aggie history that remains dear to all who go to school in College Station. The cadets took the pup back to campus with them and, against regulations, let her sleep in the dormitory. When reveille sounded the next morning, the dog let out a howl of disapproval and she was known ever more as Reveille.

She soon had free run of all campus facilities and was known to attend a chemistry class now and an English lecture then. A cadet who discovered Reveille asleep in his bunk made other arrangements for the night—usually on the floor. Reveille came to recognize the cadet uniform and befriended all who wore it.

At the Texas game of 1931, Reveille debuted as the official Texas A&M mascot by leading the famous Aggie Band onto the field.

A pep rally before the 1931 battle with the Aggies attracts a crowd in Austin.

The privileges of Reveille I included joining the cadets at mess and leading the band at halftime. The highly regarded mascot even had her own seat on trains.

Both teams were 6–3 for the year; Texas that season had made its first football foray into the sport's northern stronghold since its ill-fated attack on Chicago in 1904, and Harvard sent the 'Horns reeling back to the Southwest with a 35–7 licking.

In what *The Battalion* described as "the classic of classics," Texas' Ernie Koy scored a touchdown but Ox Blanton missed on the extra-point attempt. An Aggie six-pointer by G.C. "Frenchy" Domingue, plus the point-after, gave A&M a one-point victory, and Reveille earned her biscuits. 🏈

1932

"True Texas Orange"

The Longhorn football team was in its fifth year of wearing the burnt orange jerseys now so familiar to Texas fans. Clyde Littlefield had introduced them, replacing the light orange shirts that tended to fade to yellow after a few washings. The shade became lighter again during World War II because of a shortage of dye. Controversy over the use of burnt orange continued until 1966, when a chancellor's committee ruled it was true "Texas Orange," but bright orange is still used for most other school functions.

Bohn Hilliard, Harrison Stafford, and Ernie Koy were the backbone of one of the strongest backfields in Texas history. Only those three, along with one Baylor player, cracked a TCU-dominated All-Southwest Conference list. The 'Horns would finish the year at 5–1 in the league, good enough for second place behind the undefeated Horned Frogs. At A&M, where the student population now totaled 1,995, Madison Bell had already begun to feel the heat; his 1–2–2 conference mark would raise the temperature considerably.

The A&M cadets did not parade before the game in Austin, but the Goodyear blimp *Reliance* made an appearance. And Bevo II was on the sideline. Through all the excitement, Texas swamped the visitors, 21–0. 🏈

Matty Bell's first 1929 A&M team boasted no line-man weighing more than 180 pounds; the heaviest backs weighed 170 pounds.

1933

Musical Coaches

When SMU scored its last touchdown in a 19–0 triumph over A&M at College Station on November 11, Mustang line coach Russell McIntosh said to head coach Ray Morrison, "I'm afraid that will finish Matty down here." McIntosh was right. Within three months Matty Bell had McIntosh's job.

While Arkansas was winning its first SWC title, A&M and Texas were muddling about in the middle of the standings. They had 6–3 and 4–5–1 records, respectively, before Thanksgiving. UT's Clyde Littlefield said, "The team appears in wonderful spirits but I don't believe it has much chance to win." Apparently, Texas fans felt the same way and few students made the trip to College Station. Bell had already resigned under pressure, although the Aggies were heavy favorites to top Texas.

Harry Mayne, a Texas sub who had played no more than twenty minutes all year, went in for only two plays against A&M, kicking a field goal and a point-after-touchdown to en-

sure a 10–10 tie. Still, Texas failed to avoid its first losing season in forty years of playing the game. The university's athletic council voted to retain Littlefield as coach, but he resigned to devote himself to the track program, in which his teams would win twenty-five SWC titles in forty-one seasons.

The SMU Mustangs had lacked a goal line punch, and the weakness was blamed on Russell McIntosh. He was demoted to freshman coach, and Bell was named to replace him as line coach. When SMU head coach Ray Morrison left SMU after the 1934 season to go to Vanderbilt, he took McIntosh with him, and Bell replaced Morrison, after six seasons at TCU and five at A&M.

Aggie officials couldn't help but notice coach Homer Norton, whose Centenary College teams had given the Aggies fits while compiling a 13–13–2 record against SWC schools over the years. The Shreveport, Louisiana, school would base its repeated applications for SWC membership on this evidence of athletic equality, but league fathers politely declined every year. Norton got into the SWC without the Gentlemen, however, when A&M hired him to replace Bell.

1934

Chevigny Steps Out

Jack Chevigny was only three games into his first year as Texas football coach when he presented the school with one of its grandest moments in athletics. His Steers had only edged Texas Tech and beaten the Texas freshman squad when they took on Notre Dame, Chevigny's alma mater, at South Bend. Chevigny, an Indiana native with a reputation for toughness, had scored a touchdown for the Irish in Notre Dame's famous game "for the Gipper." Upon taking the Texas job for $4,200 a year, he converted the Texas T into the Notre Dame box shift offense. Notre Dame hadn't lost an opening game since 1896 and didn't expect to in 1934. Texas was offered $5,000 just to show up.

In his pre-game speech, Chevigny told his players about the immortal Notre Dame coach Knute Rockne, and about his own dying father and his mother buried nearby. Chevigny claimed Rockne had wanted him to become the Irish coach but, when the Rock was killed in an airplane crash, Chevigny's

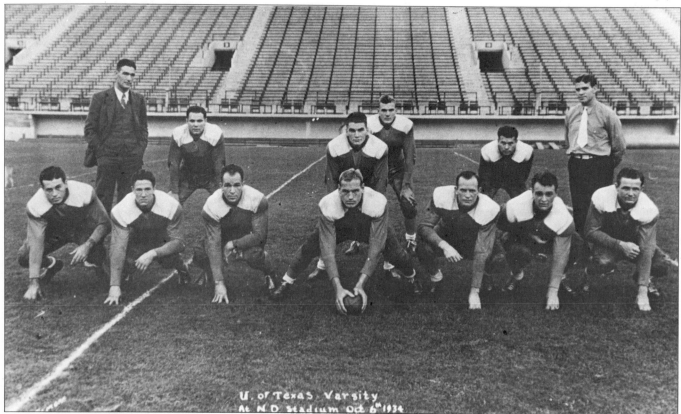

The 1934 Texas Longhorns line up in Notre Dame Stadium the day before they upset the Irish 7–6. Coach Jack Chevigny is at left, and assistant coach Ed Olle stands opposite, to the right of running back Bohn Hilliard.

"Hullabaloo, Canek! Canek!" Cadets turn out in force for the 1934 game in Austin. When asked to translate the chorus from the Aggie War Hymn, one cadet volunteered: "Beat the hell out of Texas University."

hopes to coach at his alma mater died, too. Apparently moved by their coach's sentiment, the 'Horns recovered a Notre Dame fumble on the opening kickoff, and three plays later Bohn Hilliard scored the touchdown that led to a 7–6 upset. Scarcely more than 100 miles away, in Lafayette, Indiana, powerhouse Purdue was upset by Rice, 14–0, on the same day. It was a Saturday that established the Southwest Conference as a football league.

In College Station, Homer Norton was struggling. In five years, he would produce a national championship squad that remains the best in Aggie history, but he was a long way from such glory in 1934. "Homer was such a fine gentleman and commanded a lot of respect," Dana Bible said later. "His teams were always sound, well-conditioned and had a jaw-to-jaw, toe-to-toe attitude. Homer often had a surprise for you, but I found he was always generous in defeat and humble in victory."

On Thanksgiving, one day after A&M won the first of thirty-five games played between freshman teams of the two schools (it would win only eight more), Texas ambushed the Aggies, 13–0, at Memorial Stadium. Jack Chevigny had started well. 🏈

1935

The Other Schools Shine

A&M beat Texas 20–6 on Turkey Day in 1935, but both schools ate crow in the month before: they would finish in a dead heat for last place in the SWC. Each team had won only one game, Texas having beaten Baylor.

This was, instead, the year of Southern Methodist and Texas Christian. Two days after the A&M-Texas game, a sellout crowd watched the biggest blowout of a football fight ever played in the Southwest. Matty Bell had his former employers scratching their heads as he brought his first team at SMU into the TCU game with a 10–0 record.

Dutch Meyer's second group of Horned Frogs also stood 10–0. When the two squared off in Fort Worth, it was for a Rose Bowl invitation. The SMU-TCU rivalry heated to new temperatures as Dallas and Fort Worth rallied behind their respective colleges. Sports writers from all over the United States, including Grantland Rice, attended. TCU's stadium couldn't hold the crowd in its 30,000 seats. Fans not in the stadium were treated to the first broadcast by radio network from the Southwest.

The Frogs poured onto the field with great excitement, jumping all over each other, in some contrast to their opponents' entrance. The SMU players walked onto the field like professional mourners. But behind All-America selections Truman Spain, tackle, J. C. Wetsel, guard, and the great Bobby Wilson in the backfield, the Mustangs got off to a 14–0 lead in the early going; TCU pulled to within a touchdown by halftime.

At intermission, Bell said one sentence to his players, a statement that would become famous: "You have 30 minutes to play and a lifetime to think about it." TCU showed off its

UT team captain Joe Brevard Smartt discusses strategy with coach Jack Chevigny, 1935.

two All-America choices in the second half —with "Slingin' Sammy" Baugh throwing and center Darrell Lester doing the line work, the Frogs evened the game at 14–14 in the final quarter. SMU then faked a punt at their own thirty-seven and threw a touch-down pass.

SMU took its 20–14 victory and a 24–0 trampling of A&M the following week into the Rose Bowl, where Stanford marred the Mus-tangs' record, 7–0. TCU edged Louisiana State by 3–2 in the Sugar Bowl. SMU and TCU, who between them landed ten players on the thirteen-man all-conference list, basked in the warm, new spotlight shining on Southwest Conference football. It was bleak for them in 1935, but within the decade of the '30s, the Texas Aggies would feel the warmth.

"Texas Fight." University yell leaders, 1935.

1936

High Finance, Low Results

In 1933, the year before Homer Hill Norton became the Texas A&M coach, the athletic association had had to scrape to pay the interest on its $210,000 stadium mortgage. By the time Norton departed after fourteen seasons in College Station, he was able to leave the athletic association a surplus of more than $250,000.

In his first year, Norton had found some alumni to persuade the state legislature to pass an act permitting the college to lend the athletic association $30,000. That took care of the 1934 interest on the mortgage. But in 1935, the interest money just wasn't there, the stadium bonds went into default, and the bank took over the budget. Norton's third year brought yet another default, and the coach was hospitalized for surgery on stomach ulcers. In 1937, Norton gambled by persuading the bank to lend the athletic association another $25,000 for scholarships. Finally, with those, he talked thirty-seven of the state's top forty high school players into Aggie uniforms. Among those thirty-seven were eventual All-America selections John Kimbrough, Marshall Robnett and Joe Routt, plus All-SWC stars Herb Smith, Jim Sterling, Jim Thomason, and Ernie Pannell. The bank's money, at last, was safe.

Norton didn't have that kind of talent in 1936, but he still managed to direct the Aggies to eight wins in twelve games, including an 18–7 decision that knocked TCU out of the conference title. TCU had beaten Santa Clara, the nation's only remaining undefeated, untied team, and would defeat Marquette in the Cotton Bowl.

Jack Chevigny's Longhorns fell to 1–5 (2–6–1 overall in 1936), but the lone conference victory was an important one, a 7–0 contest against the Aggies at Memorial Stadium. ◗

Joe Routt became A&M's first All-America selection in 1936, and the honor was repeated in 1937.

Dana Bible returns to Texas as Longhorn coach, 1937.

1937

Bible's Second Edition

Dana Bible had been paid $2,400 a year coaching A&M to a combined 24 – 1 – 1 mark in 1917, 1918, and 1919. In 1937, Texas wanted Bible, then at Nebraska, so badly that he was offered a twenty-year contract, the first ten as coach and athletic director, the second ten as athletic director only, at $15,000 a year. As such a contract would mean that Bible would earn more than the university president, the legislators stepped in to solve the problem by giving the president a raise—and Bible became Texas' twenty-first football coach.

"When D. X. returned to Texas," Frank Anderson remembered, "there were four people waiting for him at the station. One T.U. man and three Aggies, one of them me." Bible promptly predicted a title team in five years. He immediately put into effect "the Bible Plan," by which alumni were responsible for recruiting Texas high school players. But first, Bible had to deal with 1937, the first year that the Texas Tower was illuminated in orange after football victories. The Tower was so lighted but twice in 1937—a season that must have been painful to Bible, a man

whose Nebraska teams had lost only three conference games in his eight years there.

Meanwhile, at A&M, 1937 gate receipts and the 1938 advance sales met the interest due on Kyle Field, covered the most recent $25,000 bank loan, and restored the budget to Homer Norton. Snow fell two days before Thanksgiving, but the field at A&M, kept under a tarp, was in good shape and the weather on game day was clear and warm. The Aggies won Bible's own homecoming game, 7 – 0. But the new Texas coach would have his day; the man who had worked so hard to keep the Kyle Field jinx alive would soon be the man to shatter it. 🏈

1938

How to Save a Season

The Farmers in Hell
by Marie Rienta

Listen my children while I relate
The tale of the farmers' terrible fate.
'Twas on that famous Turkey Day
The Texas Aggies journeyed our way.

"Texas can't win"—people jeered at the
  thought.
A season of football had gone for naught.

The Longhorns had been beaten 10 times in
  a row
Yet loyal supporters still shouted, "Yea, Texas, let's go."

The air was filled with the music of bands,
Great shouts of enthusiasm came up from the
  stands.
The greatest war of all wars was about to
  begin,
A war that was waged between twenty-two
  men.

Gilly Davis took the kick-off—made a beau-
  tiful run.
He twisted and scampered, shifted and spun,
A touchdown march was well under way.
Longhorns fight hard and long 'til the last
  minute of play.
Watch Wally Lawson speed down that field
And look at that A&M Aggie line yield.
Come on boys one more down and it's over.
Say Aggies, were you going to plant steers—
  or clover?

The Steers have really gone out on a tear.
They're scattering the farmers everywhere;
Look at Charlie Naiser stop Todd in his
  tracks,
This isn't just fiction, (we hope), it's real
  facts. . . .

Many victories for Texas will follow this one
  Thursday,

Cadets depart for Austin, 1938. Those who did not make the trip held the traditional yell practice at the train station.

And the Longhorn team will again hold full sway.
How do I know all of this to be true,
My Bible told me—didn't yours tell you??

Despite the rhymes of undergraduate poets, 1938 was as lousy a year for Texas as it was for the Aggies. In fact, to try to ensure that the Longhorns would not suffer a winless season, the students' assembly passed the Aggie Adjustment Act (to Annihilate Antagonizing Aggies), which purported to limit the Aggies in the amount of yards they could gain per play, the number of passes they could complete, and so on.

It—or something—worked. A&M scored its first points ever in Memorial Stadium by recovering a fumble in Texas' end zone, but its extra-point kick was blocked by Texas center Roy Baines. The PAT after Texas' lone touchdown was the only one the team converted all year, and Texas won, 7–6. Bible's second Steer squad would finish in a last-place tie with Arkansas, one step behind the Farmers in league play and miles behind L. R. "Dutch" Meyer's national champion TCU Horned Frogs—but at least they beat the Aggies. 🏈

1939

Aggie Perfection

Homer Norton called his 1939 Aggies the perfect team. It was considered a toss-up whether that A&M squad, called the "College Station Wagon," or TCU's 1938 team, the for-

ward-pass wonders of the age, was the best squad in those SWC single-platoon days. "Jarrin' Jawn" Kimbrough led the Farmers to a 10–0 season, including a 20–0 conquest of Texas, and the No. 1 national ranking.

Before the season, Norton had publicly announced that he had a team of championship caliber, spurring advance sales to the point that the athletic association paid off its six-year-old debt to the college. The January 1, 1940, Sugar Bowl pitted the Aggies against second-ranked Tulane in a showdown of incredible thrills. Norton's motto was "It's how you show up at the showdown," and the Aggies showed up a smidgen better than the Green Wave, 14–13. With the money A&M received from the bowl, Norton redeemed $120,000 of the $210,000 Kyle Field bonds, and with the advance sales for 1940 he paid off the balance. Norton's contract was torn up, and he was granted a huge salary increase.

The Aggies copped the SWC crown when SMU beat Baylor on the Saturday before Thanksgiving. The A&M players were on the practice field when they were given the news, and the tears and congratulations flowed. But before too long, somebody yelled, "Hell, we play Texas Thursday!" and they returned to work.

Texas was improving under Dana Bible's instruction, but in A&M it encountered an overland crunch it couldn't handle. And with Marshall Robnett on the line and the seemingly unstoppable Kimbrough carrying the ball, A&M brushed aside other SWC foes; only SMU came close. The Aggies totaled 112 points in conference competition and allowed only 8.

1940

The Bitterest Pill

"To Hell with the Aggies."

The sign outside the Kappa Sigma house at the University of Texas caused some trouble. The dean's request that it be removed went unheeded, and Austin citizens, including the police chief, called the school to complain that the sign was undignified. Some Aggies sent the Kappa Sigs a message of their own: "If you don't take down the sign, we'll tear it down." University "victory watchers" surrounded Littlefield Fountain on campus all night, waiting for the Aggies who were reported on their way to Austin. One A&M freshman had two teeth knocked out in a late-night scuffle on University Avenue. Although the dean ordered that the word *hell* be marked out and *censored* put in its place on the Kappa Sigma sign, Aggie raiders still came after it. About fifty of them swarmed the area, but were prevented from reaching the fraternity house by Army officers.

Such antagonism set the stage for the monumental Thanksgiving Day battle. A&M was 8–0 and hadn't lost since it last met Texas in Austin, nineteen games before. The Aggies were confident another bowl game was in their immediate future, this time the prestigious Rose Bowl. Dana Bible's ploy before this game was to read to his Texas players Edgar Guest's poem, "It Can Be Done."

The game opened with fifty-eight of the most astonishing seconds Aggies and their supporters have ever suffered. On the first play from scrimmage, Texas' Pete Layden

In fourteen years as A&M coach, Homer Norton brought his teams to three Southwest Conference championships, and to the national championship in 1939.

UT welcomed the Aggies to Austin in 1940 by snapping their longest winning streak.

Guard Marshall Robnett, third Aggie player to win All-Southwest Conference and All-America honors in both 1939 and 1940.

faked an end run and connected on a crossover pass to Jack Crain, who was downed on the A&M thirty-five. Layden failed on another pass, then faked a sweep and threw a pass to wingback Noble Doss. Doss, still known around the university as "the man who caught the pass," made an acrobatic catch as he went out of bounds at the one-yard line. Layden plunged over on the next play, and Crain kicked the point. After fifty-eight seconds, it was 7–0.

Over the remaining fifty-nine minutes of play, the Aggies and John Kimbrough kept driving toward their Rose Bowl vision, but it proved to be a mirage. "Kimbrough was one tough running back," Texas' 1922-23 yell leader and avid Longhorn fan for many decades, Arno "Shorty" Nowotny, remembered in 1980. "But their quarterback forgot how tough he was and would start throwing and we would intercept." A&M tried five long passes; all five were intercepted.

After the 7–0 loss, snapping A&M's longest winning streak, Homer Norton told his players, "This is perhaps the bitterest pill you will ever have to swallow, but there is one thing about it. If you will take what happened to you today as a lesson when you get out into life and won't get cocky and overconfident, then this defeat might not be as bad as it seems." A&M dropped from No. 1 in the national polls to No. 9, but the Farmers edged a strong Fordham team in the Cotton Bowl, 13–12. The Aggies shared the SWC crown with SMU.

The Daily Texan saw the game as an omen: "A&M will never beat Texas in Memorial Stadium," the paper proclaimed. ●

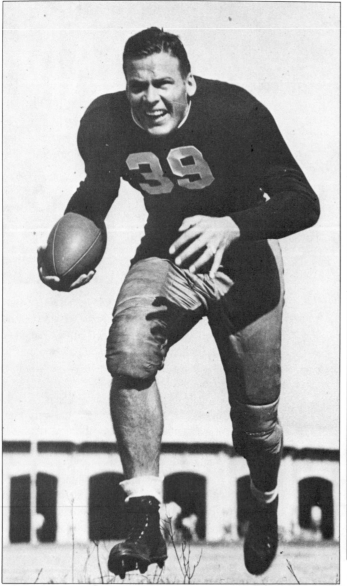

'Jarrin' Jawn" Kimbrough, selected as All-Southwest Conference and All-America in both 1939 and 1940, also carried the Aggies to a national championship, 1940.

Jim Thomason, All-Southwest Conference Aggie halfback, 1939 and 1940.

Norton's "perfect team," the 1939 national champs.

LONGHORNS WIN!!!
Holiday Declared Friday After Texans Plow Under Aggies, 7-0, in 58 Seconds

November 29, 1940.

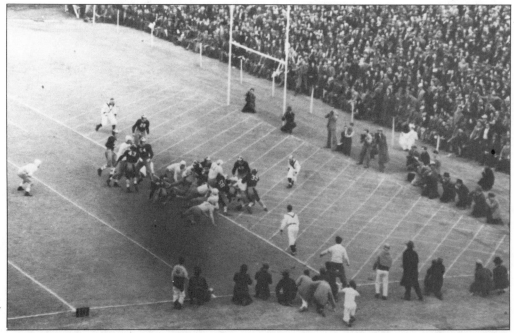

Pete Layden (11) scores a touchdown during Texas' 7–0 upset win over A&M in Memorial Stadium, 1940.

The 1931 team wears the burnt orange jerseys officially adopted by Clyde Littlefield in 1927.

I'm another "Jackass" from....A&M

Tea-Sips dressed as Aggies board the "Aggie Special" for a ride in the Orange and White Parade.

A parking problem at Kyle Field, 1935.

Founded in 1894 by a Czechoslovakian cobbler, Joseph Halick (Class of '98), the Fightin' Texas Aggie Band performs at Memorial Stadium, 1934.

Cadets march down Congress Avenue toward the state Capitol, and on to defeat in Memorial Stadium, 1940.

Students pack 3-year-old Gregory Gym to cheer the Longhorns to victory at South Bend.

THE
1940's

1941

"What Good Would It Be?"

Rarely have the football teams of A&M and Texas both been so strong as they were prior to the 1941 battle at College Station. Aggie seniors had suffered only one loss in their twenty-nine games, that to Texas. The Longhorns, for their part, led by Pete Layden and Jack Crain, the "Nocona Nugget," flattened their first seven opponents before Baylor threw a touchdown pass with eighteen seconds left and tied the 'Horns, 7–7.

In the week after the Baylor game, UT was the subject of a story-photo spread in *Life* magazine. The title was "Texas Football: A Great University Has Nation's Top Team," and *Life* reportedly became required reading for freshman English at A&M.

On the Saturday after the magazine appeared, Texas was struck by lightning for the second time. TCU coach Dutch Meyer pleaded with his players to "fight 'em until hell freezes over, and then fight 'em on the ice!" Meyer coached a defensive masterpiece, holding the highest-scoring team in the history of the SWC to one touchdown. When the Frogs completed a six-point pass with seven seconds remaining, it capped a 14–7 shocker that ranked with Texas' 7–3 stunner over A&M in 1920 among football's great upsets. After Texas stumbled, the Aggies mosied into the No. 1 spot in the nation in the unofficial ratings of the day, Texas falling to the No. 16 position.

A week after they stuck Texas, the Frogs tied Rice, 0–0, handing Texas A&M the conference title, the first time ever that one school had won the crown in consecutive years.

Before the annual showdown in College Station, Texas students burned red candles to break the Kyle Field jinx, following a Chinese custom, and one student hired a "colored mystic" to place a jinx on A&M, according to a newspaper report. Despite a peace pact between the schools' student bodies, *The Daily Texan* ran a headline reading, "A Sage Unto His Son Once Said: An Aggie Good Is an Aggie Dead," and the *Texan* editor was moved to send a letter of apology to *The Battalion* and the A&M cadets. *The Texan* also had referred to the Texas students as the univer-

Texas football makes the cover of Life *Magazine, November 17, 1941.*

Dana Bible with Jack "Nocona Nugget" Crain, who helped Texas defeat Southwest Conference champ A&M at Kyle Field, 1941.

Malcolm Kutner, UT All-America end, 1941.

The spirit of the Twelfth Man as embodied by the Aggie Band during the Thanksgiving Day halftime show, 1941.

sity's "twelfth man," and that appropriation of Aggie legend irked the Aggies. A *Battalion* editorial noted that a university pep rally had drawn but twenty-five students: "Texas university's student body, belatedly called the twelfth man, died a mortal death. . . . The name still sticks and by right of use belongs to no others than the Aggies."

Concerning the Thanksgiving Day battle, *The Battalion* pointed out, "We are undefeated and untied, and we're the champs of the Southwest Conference. But what good would it all be if we got beaten by Texas?"

What good, indeed? Texas trampled the champions 23–0 in its first Kyle Field triumph since the celebrated 1923 game. The Longhorns had their eyes on the Rose Bowl, and the bowl's officials told them they could have it if they would cancel their final regular-season game, one with Oregon. The bowl folks were afraid Texas would lose to the Ducks, who had given tough Oregon State a scare before losing, 12–7. Texas kept Oregon on their schedule, clobbered them 71–7, and passed up the bowl scene. The January 1, 1942, Rose Bowl was played in Durham, North Carolina, because large gatherings of people had been outlawed on the West Coast during the early war years, and brought together Duke and Oregon State.

Texas finished the year at fourth in the na-

tion, A&M landed in ninth place. 🏈

1942

Aunt Emma's Delight

"The Aggies and Longhorns," wrote the *Austin American*'s Wilbur Hart, "have played one another about half a hundred times and the consequences always have been something you could write about to Aunt Emma, except that she was probably there and saw it herself."

During wartime, the fighting between Texas' premier football schools reached new heights. Two cadets set fire to Texas' bonfire on a Tuesday night. The first of hundreds of enraged university students to arrive at the scene chased the pair across a field, but the culprits escaped. Making do, the Texas student body came on out, at about 11:30 p.m., and watched the blaze, premature by twenty-one hours or so.

Two days later, Aunt Emma and everybody saw A&M score its first earned touchdown in Memorial Stadium when Barney Welch picked up his own fumble on a punt return and scooted seventy-one yards. Texas' Jackie Field scored from twelve yards out, though, with fifty seconds remaining for a 12–6

Longhorn win, giving Texas the conference crown. It was Texas' fourth title, compared to the eight the Aggies had garnered—despite Texas' 15–11–2 lead in their own series—since 1915.

A thousand miles to the east, Georgia Tech ended its regular season by getting trampled 34–0 by Georgia. Tech coach Bill Alexander, in the hospital after a heart attack, predicted such an outcome because his Yellow Jackets were worn out after a remarkable year; Bobby Dodd filled in as coach for the game. Afterwards, Alexander got a call in his hospital room. "Aleck, this is D. X. Bible calling from Austin. We've been named for the Cotton Bowl and want to play you and Georgia Tech. Will you accept?"

Alexander responded, "D. X., have you heard what the score was today? It was 34–0—the worst licking Georgia has given us in 40 years."

"I know the score," Bible said, "and I know your team. It has been one of the best in the country this year and will be again on January 1. Our people out here want to see Georgia Tech and I want to play you. The Cotton Bowl will be filled."

The Yellow Jackets may have been one of the best in the country, but they weren't the best in the Cotton Bowl in 1943—Alexander watched from the bench as Tech lost to Texas, 14–7. 🏈

Billy "Rooster" Andrews perches on Jim Plyler (left) and Harlan Wetz. As a freshman, the waterboy-turned-kicker was sent by a group of seniors to capture an escaped fighting cock, and so gained his nickname.

1943

"Rooster" Steps Forth

The war thinned the ranks of all colleges, but few were so bereft of gridiron talent as Texas A&M. The team that remained after the nation's call to arms was A&M's youngest ever, with an average age of seventeen. Still, Homer Norton's tenth A&M squad avoided defeat through its first four conference encounters. (Baylor withdrew from football competition in 1943 and 1944 because of the war, and the league had but six schools going for the flag.)

The University of Texas also sent thousands of young men into the service, but then it had more to give. And it was left with more of a football team. Except for a 14–7 upset loss to Southwestern, the Longhorns pretty well mashed their six other challengers. Norton dared D. X. Bible to play only his "Texas high school boys" against his youthful Aggies; Bible declined.

In Texas' game with TCU, UT waterboy Billy "Rooster" Andrews kicked himself into the limelight and became a hero. Bible had spotted the diminutive Andrews drop-kicking field goals during a practice. In the 46–7 rout of the Frogs, Bible asked the popular waterboy if he wanted to try his foot at scoring a point or two for the team. Andrews donned a uniform, kicked two extra points, and was a campus hero by Monday.

Some of the Army boys in training at A&M came to dislike the cadets and asked to sit with the Texas students, but A&M officials declined. Among the 7,300 Navy, Marine, and Army Air Force trainees stationed in College Station and required to sit with the Aggies were several UT exes; the result was a "Beat the Aggies" banner unfurled in the heart of the A&M Navy section. A&M's cadet corps piled from the stands en masse and thundered toward the middies. Although cadet corps officers intervened and ordered the Aggies to their seats, the banner disappeared in the rush.

Texas had gained 237 yards per game rushing during the year, and A&M's Kiddie Korps had held opponents to 52 yards per game on the ground. After Texas took a 13–0 lead, the Aggies came back to tie it at 13–13. Texas punched into A&M territory, but the cadets in the stands stirred up such noise that the Steers failed three times in a row to run one play. Texas took the lead by the half, however, and the cadets were quieted somewhat by the 27–13 final score.

Texas' team had to acquire the university naval commander's approval to attend the Cotton Bowl, where a 7–7 tie with Randolph Field resulted. A&M accepted an Orange Bowl invitation to play LSU, which had lost to the Aggies 28–13 during the regular season; on January 1, LSU paid them back, 19–14.

1944

So Fine!

Everything about the A&M-Texas rivalry was fine in 1944. D. X. Bible thought all was fine, as did his quarterback, seventeen-year-old Bobby Layne. Even Homer Norton noted the fineness of the occasion. Six Aggies did a fine job, for example, of painting "Yea, Aggies" across Memorial Stadium's press box on the Sunday preceding the big game. They also scrawled "Beat the hell out of Tea U." on Austin fraternity and sorority houses, and only a night watchman on the twenty-sixth floor of the Texas Tower kept them from desecrating that particular shrine.

The Texan and *The Battalion* pleaded for peace among students. "Bitterest fight on record," reported the *Texan*, "goes back to a baseball game when a Texas fan started a series of fist fights by throwing tomatoes at Aggie fans." The game itself evoked memories of the remarkable Texas win in 1940, which

Joe Parker, UT All-America end, 1943.

saved the Memorial Stadium "tradition." A&M's players dedicated the 1944 game to their mascot, Reveille, who had died the previous January. A&M's Paul Yates, the SWC's leading rusher, returned the opening kickoff out of the end zone and was clobbered by 285-pound Harland Weitz at the two-yard line. A&M immediately punted and Roger Evans returned to the visitors' thirty-five. Texas' first play was a double handoff plus a basket pass back to Bobby Layne, who then threw to freshman right end Jim Watson, who was tackled at the A&M nine. Aggie rushers had Layne boxed in as he looked for a receiver on the next play, but he swept down the sideline and then cut back, dragging his tackler into the end zone. The score: 6–0.

In the fourth quarter, A&M got the ball at Texas' forty-four. Two passes airlifted the Aggies to the twelve, and three running plays netted a first down at the two. Texas end Hubert Bechtol, wearing his "man-from-Mars" headgear to protect a broken jaw, and Leroy Anderson, who had his own jaw broken after intercepting a fourth-quarter Aggie pass, were both in the lineup that held the Aggies for no gain on first and second downs. A&M's third play lost two yards. On fourth-and-four, the Aggies tried a sweep, fumbled, and recovered on the fourteen—threat ended, Memorial Stadium tradition preserved.

Bible: "That's a fine old tradition we have, and the boys did a fine job of maintaining it. Our boys played a fine game, that was a fine goal line stand at the finish, the A&M boys played a fine game and it was a fine victory. Everything's fine."

Norton: "Texas had a fine team and we had a fine team. It was a fine game."

Layne: "Happiest darn day of my life!"

For three consecutive years, UT end Hub Bechtol was both an All-Southwest Conference and All-America selection, 1944–1946.

Austin businesses supported Longhorns with a two-page ad in The Daily Texan, *1944.*

"Happiest darn day of my life." UT quarterback Bobby Layne propelled the 'Horns to a 6–0 victory against A&M, 1944.

1945

Yellowbellies Triumphant

On August 6, the United States dropped the bomb on Hiroshima. On November 29, Bobby Layne dropped the bomb on Texas A&M.

On game day, Nazi war criminals were viewing films of the horrors of German concentration camps at the Nuremberg trials. Their reactions ranged from tears to curt indifference. But nobody in Kyle Field's stands was indifferent to what they were seeing. At stake was the SWC title, which Texas could win outright or share with A&M or three other teams. The contest marked only the fifth time that Texas and A&M were still in the running for the crown by Thanksgiving. The Steers had lost to their long-time nemesis, Rice, and the Farmers had lost two of five SWC skirmishes. The game had been a sellout for more than a month. Thousands of Aggie grads, fed up with the recent trend in the big game were home from the war demanding that the "Yellowbellies" be whipped. For the fans who came up from Austin, a round-trip bus ticket was $4.37.

Ralph Ellsworth put Texas ahead by seven points with an early eighty-one-yard gallop, but the Aggies tied it up by the half. They carved a 10–7 fourth-quarter lead before a

Texas punt hit Aggie Preston Smith on the leg and the 'Horns recovered at A&M's two. George Graham scored the touchdown, but the snap went awry on the point-after. Down 13–10, the Aggies moved to midfield but faltered, and Bobby Layne hit Peppy Blount with a long pass to widen Texas' lead. Former waterboy Rooster Andrews faked a kick on the point after and passed to Layne for the single point that made the final score 20–10. As Cotton Bowl representative, Texas defeated Missouri, 40–27.

After the season, Homer Norton underwent stomach surgery. Eventually, he lost 80 percent of his stomach. To ease the strain of coaching, he invented his "coaching sky buggy," which was the body of an old coupe atop a fifteen-foot steel scaffold, from which Norton instructed his team through a loudspeaker. Frank Leahy at Notre Dame had one built, Paul "Bear" Bryant would use one later at Alabama, and soon, Norton's invention became a coaching commonplace.

1946

At Least They Scored

The story of Heman Marion Sweatt wasn't about football, but it charged the emotions at Texas A&M and the University of Texas about

as much as the annual grid clash between the two. Sweatt wanted to study law at Texas, but had made the mistake of being born black. Equal educational opportunities for Negroes was one thing but no one with any sense, as *The Texan* editorialized, was advocating that blacks be allowed to attend the state institutions now populated solely by whites. On the Wednesday before the A&M-Texas game, the Texas Legislature approved the establishment of a first-year law course for Negroes to be held in Austin until the opening of the Houston campus that would become known as Texas Southern; Sweatt would become, in his first year, its only student.

Problems were arising in athletics by this time, too, and the issue was as simple as black and white. The University of Miami had canceled its game with Penn State because the Lions had two Negro players; A&M and Texas were still quite a few years from fielding black football players.

The 1946 encounter between the two teams was Dana Bible's final game as Texas coach. Rice, which had again beaten Texas, would win the SWC title this year, but by Thanksgiving the 'Horns still had a shot at tying for the championship. To set the stage again: A&M's offense had never scored a touchdown in Memorial Stadium. Barney Welch's punt return in 1942, a recovered fumble in the end zone four years earlier, and five points earned in 1926 constituted the whole of the Aggies' Memorial Stadium out-

The 'Horns edge A&M.

1947

Norton's Farewell

"An innovation of the 1947 football classic," reported the *Austin American-Statesman*, "is special air flights [to College Station]. Dig a canal between Austin and College Station and it would probably overflow with traffic on Turkey Day."

Racial tension in athletics had begun to overflow into the state of Texas. Arizona State College was asked by the Texas School of Mines and West Texas State to leave its two outstanding black ball carriers, Morrison Warren and George Diggs, at home when ASC traveled to El Paso and Canyon for games.

Heman Marion Sweatt, 1946.

put. Their win-loss record at Memorial was by now 0–11.

By dusk on November 28, 1946, that record clicked to 0–12. Bobby Layne and All-America end Hubert Bechtol commanded the Longhorns to a 24–0 lead before A&M chiseled a small nick in the granite-like Memorial Stadium tradition by scoring a touchdown from scrimmage. The 24–7 final was a record seventh straight win over A&M for Texas, and 200th lifetime victory for Bible against 74 losses and 23 ties. After the game, Bible said of his players, "They said they were glad they could give me a good parting gift, and I know of no nicer gift they could have given me than this." As per his 1937 contract, Bible retired as coach but remained athletic director for ten more years.

Aggie alumni were calling for Norton's scalp. He had three years left on a five-year contract, but he hadn't beaten Texas since 1939. 🏈

The all-white Texas Aggies were out of the running in SWC warfare by game day, but Texas, under new coach Blair Cherry, still hoped to tie with SMU for the title. SMU had beaten the Steers 14–13, but Texas had trampled its eight other opponents, including Arkansas, in the only SWC game ever played in Tennessee (at Memphis). Back in Austin, the fire department threw cold water on Texas yell leader Barefoot Sanders' plans to ignite Texas spirit. Firefighters held the "hazardous" bonfire to "little more than a smudgepot."

Similarly, the Longhorns held A&M to little in the way of scoring. Fullback Tom Landry scored the first of five Texas touchdowns en route to a 32–13 victory, Texas' fourth straight at Kyle Field after so many winless

A&M ad in the 1949 football program.

Tom Landry, UT fullback, scored the first touchdown in the 1947 game against A&M.

years there. The achievement put Texas in the Sugar Bowl against Alabama, for Texas' fourth post-season bowl appearance. That bowl game, a 27–7 decision in favor of the Longhorns, was one of a record four post-season contests involving Southwest Conference teams that year. Cotton Bowl visitor Penn State tied 13–13 with league champ SMU, whose brilliant Doak Walker nudged out Texas' Bobby Layne for All-America honors.

At year's end, Aggie alumni and officials overlooked Homer Norton's overall 82–53–9 record because it included a 3–11 mark against A&M's biggest rival, and paid Norton $20,000 for the last two years on his contract. He retired, and later ran a restaurant across the street from the main campus entrance until his death in 1965. A&M named Harry Stiteler coach; he'd have a rough time of it, too. 🏈

1948

A&M Wins, 14–14

After dark on Sunday, November 21, a two-seater plane buzzed the Texas A&M campus at an altitude of about seventy-five feet. According to the most reliable report, the plane passed over the Aggies' precious bonfire six times. On the first five runs, jugs of gasoline with incendiary flares attached were dropped toward the wood pile. The third explosive ignited the stack, but cadets on guard snuffed out the blaze.

En route home from his sortie, the pilot had to put down in a field because his plane had run out of gas; he refueled from an unused bomb. Upon landing at the Austin airport, from which he had "borrowed" the

plane, the Texas student, a combat veteran, was met by his dean and immediately suspended from school. At a campus fraternity house, a spokesman admitted his group had collected money for the raid. "Reprisals are expected," he said, "since the Aggies have learned the name of our fraternity, but the whole freshman football team has offered to be our guards." Revenge came in expected fashion. Littlefield Fountain blushed with red paint one morning. On Wednesday night, Austin police got calls every ten minutes about student fights or disturbances.

As for the game, Aggie revenge after eight years of Texas domination was not expected. Texas saw a chance to win half the SWC trophy, again with SMU; A&M saw little chance of anything. The Farmers were winless after nine games (the worst record of any team in the history of the conference) under Harry Stiteler, who in his first two years as coach would not win one conference game.

"Tradition Trembles in Steer-Aggie Tie," the *Statesman* headline would read the next morning. Eight times Texas moved deep into A&M territory but scored only twice. Typically, the last-place team in the conference was the league's "passingest" squad; this year the honor went to A&M. Down by a 14–7 count in the fourth quarter, the Aggies went for the bomb. A Buryl Baty aerial intended for Charlie Royalty was batted by two Texas defenders who collided in the air, as Aggie Charlie Wright snared the ball at the Texas twenty-eight and scored.

The resulting 14–14 tie was "as good as a victory for us," Stiteler said. The result knocked the 'Horns out of a first-place tie with the SMU Mustangs, who for the second straight year had their grip on the crown loosened somewhat by a tie game with TCU two days after Thanksgiving. Texas was invited to the Orange Bowl, however, and decked Georgia. 🏈

1949

The Rivalry Flares Up

The Aggies had a hard Thanksgiving week, and the game with Texas was the least of it.

Sunday: A carload of Aggies cruised up to Texas' bonfire, intending to drench it with gasoline and ignite it with a match. All that caught fire, though, was the back seat of their

"For we are the Aggies—the Aggies so true. We're from Texas A.M.U."

car and the Aggies sitting therein. Two A&M students were hospitalized with severe burns.

Tuesday: Determined Aggies bribed a truck driver to help them. The driver backed his truck up to the UT bonfire with a load of wood and three bombs hidden in the cargo. The bombs fizzled, and two more cadets visited a hospital with gasoline burns.

An A&M student assembly representative, meanwhile, proclaimed that the "hate" between the two schools was "totally unfounded and more legend than actuality." The assembly member obviously didn't check the hospital admissions lists. The lone sparkle during the week for the Aggies was a 13–0 win in the annual freshman game at Austin. It was A&M's first victory ever in Memorial Stadium.

Texas was forced to consider the game with A&M as its "bowl game" for the year after losing to Rice, SMU, and TCU by a total of four points. The Aggies had notched a win over Texas Tech, but otherwise were as worthless as in 1948. Members of the 1909 Farmer squad were honored at the Thanksgiving clash. They had played for Charley "I Didn't Come Here to Lose" Moran and constituted the only Aggie squad ever to beat

Texas twice in one season. The hate that was "more legend than actuality" showed up on the field when Texas end Ray Stone slugged A&M's All-Southwest Conference running star, Bob Smith, in the jaw. "I was provoked," Stone said. Smith was knocked out. Stone was thrown out. The Aggies were blown out, 42–14. ●

1950

Plant You Now, Bury Us Later

The cadets of 1950 showed unusual creativity in the pranks department and met with more than the Aggies' usual success. One group sowed Memorial Stadium's turf with oats and fertilized them so that after the first rain they would spring up and spell *A and M*. Stadium workers found out and tried to eradicate the plantings, but only managed to make a dent in one letter. In 1950, at least, A&M made a name for itself in Texas' stadium.

Coach Blair Cherry, who was known as a

brilliant football tactician, was hospitalized for stomach ulcers and missed his final game, his retirement having been forced by poor health and his 1–3 mark against Oklahoma. Cherry would be listed as one of the university's most successful coaches, his overall record 32–10–1, but his most important legacy was a 3–0–1 record over the Aggies. On Thanksgiving Eve, 10,000 attended a rally in Austin and heard Arno Nowotny, yell leader back in 1922, cry, "Let's win this one for Coach Cherry!" Fred Williams, *American* sportswriter, concurred in a long, emotional column the next morning. Winning cars in the UT parade that week depicted Aggies taking a weekly bath and guarding a bale of hay.

Oklahoma had inflicted the only loss on Texas, rated No. 3 in the nation by one poll, No. 4 by the other. The Aggies had improved to 6–3 under Harry Stiteler and already had accepted an invitation to play Georgia in the President's Cup game in Maryland. The Longhorns added icing to their SWC title by whipping the Aggies 17–0, and strolled a bit too easily into the Cotton Bowl, where Tennessee took the cake, 20–14. A&M, meanwhile, won its bowl battle in Stiteler's final game as coach, 40–20. ●

1942 football program.

The University Co-op handed out schedules to make customers happy.

Members of former A&M squads urge the team on.

Bevo III, a "rip-snorting, fence-busting steer," served as the Longhorn mascot for three years before being retired to the San Antonio Zoo.

1950's

1951

"The Dirtiest Bunch Ever"

Morris Williams of the *Austin American* sports staff wrote the game story:

> Kyle Field, College Station, Nov. 29 —It was all sweetness and good fellowship just before the battle here this sunny afternoon. People from different sections of the state were nodding pleasantly to each other, the sun had shushed all the clouds out of the sky— gently, of course—and when the reverend gave the invocation and prayed for peace and good will in the world, he didn't exclude the Texases. The band played the national anthem and the A&Ms and the Texases arose and stood peacefully elbow to elbow.
>
> And then somebody put a football between two echelons of highly strung Americans. It turned out to be a mistake, because peace and good will flew out of the almost-horseshoe stadium with the speed of sound. One wise old turtle dove fathomed the sonic barriers ere he cleared the north wall.

Bob Smith, Aggie All-America, 1950.

"I'm sorry I lost that one. It's like losing a relative." Coach Edwin Price laments the 22–21 loss to A&M, 1951.

And then someone put a typewriter between the two hands of the overwrought Mr. Williams. It turned out to be a mistake, obviously, but it well describes the Thanksgiving Day action. The Aggies had the narrowest of leads late in the game when a Dan Page pass hit receiver Don Barton and Aggie defender Glenn Lippman at the same time, and Texas was credited with the completion at A&M's twenty-three. Texas tried a field goal from there with ten seconds left; it fell short and a fight erupted on the field. Cadets swarmed out of the stands for old times' sake.

Texas players offered bouquets after A&M's 22–21 win: "They were the dirtiest bunch I ever played against." Said new Texas Coach Ed Price: "I'm sorry I lost that one. It's like losing a relative."

1952

Fifty Straight for Louis Lenz

"I never heard anybody refer to the 'Aggie Spirit' without a little flow of warmth in his voice," George Sessions Perry had written in that *Post* story in 1951. "For the Aggie spirit actually is a living thing, shot through with a remarkably durable, blue-blazing conviction."

He mentioned an A&M professor of English who, in 1910, had made the mistake of betting on the University of Texas against the Aggies, then found himself besieged by most of the student body, which wanted to rough him up a bit. And Louis Lenz stood as an example of that conviction in 1952. A 1907 graduate of A&M, Lenz stood at his fiftieth straight A&M-Texas battle. On the other side, Clyde Littlefield viewed his thirty-eight in succession. They were part of the greatest crowd in the history of the series. In addition to the 64,000 ticket-buyers, a television audience brought the total number of viewers to about 250,000. Sportswriters would whine in their game stories that they shivered in the windy, forty-degree weather while announcers worked next door in a heated room.

Texas, ranked tenth and eighth in the national polls, totaled 464 yards on the ground against the Aggies, whose second-year coach, Ray George, was leading them to his second year of losing play. Texas came back from its worst modern-day defeat—49–20 to Oklahoma—and a 14–3 loss to Notre Dame to sweep the SWC. A&M fell to Texas, 32–12, propelling the Austinites into the Cotton Bowl, where they beat up Tennessee. ●

1953

Return of the Red Candles

"Once they caught several cadets from Texas A&M, the rival school out in the boon-docks, marauding around the campus at night, and summoned aid from the whole dormitory; they shaved the Aggies' heads, painted them in orange and white enamel,

In response to shotgun blasts fired by Oklahoma Rufnecks, mechanical engineering students at UT built a cannon. "Old Smokey" is fired by the Texas Cowboys whenever Texas scores.

paraded them at close drill around the intra-mural field, and in an unexpected burst of Christian charity sent them home in time for reveille."

The words are those of Willie Morris, from a chapter of *North Toward Home* in which he describes his fellow dormitory residents at the university in the mid-1950s. Morris was no doubt describing the night of Wednesday, November 25, 1953. The eleven mischievous visitors had painted *AGGIES* on a university building before being caught while painting some lawn furniture a lovely maroon. *The Texan* continues the narrative: A Texas student "delivered the welcoming address and emphasized the need of closer fellowship between TU and A&M." The newspaper added that the offenders were tossed into Littlefield Fountain after they'd been painted, and when they tried to leave, their car wouldn't start. A second group of Aggies was nabbed at 3:00 a.m., the festivities were re-enacted, and they drove away at 5:15 a.m., yelling, "We'll be back!"

The university's football team roared back from its only league loss of the year (to co-champ Rice) and had a 4–1 SWC mark by late November. The Texas students had un-boxed their red candles for Baylor, ranked No. 3 in the nation. The red-candle whammy had been used only once since the 1941 A&M game, in 1950 when the Steers upset top-ranked SMU. When Baylor students heard about the plan in 1953, they lit up every green candle in the city of Waco as a counter-whammy. Baylor's backfield, known as the "Fearsome Foursome," was a fumbling foursome against the 'Horns. Two of the four bobbles lost led to Texas scores, and red waxed green, 21–20. Twenty days later, Texas snuffed out A&M, 21–12, to share the league title, but it was Rice that downed Alabama in the Cotton Bowl. Ray George quietly exited the A&M coaching position; his successor, Paul "Bear" Bryant, came on rather more noisily.

Ray Morrison, SMU's outstanding coach from 1922 to 1934, presents Dana Bible with the Amos Alonzo Stagg Award for long service to the game, 1953.

Ray George lasted three years as Aggie head coach, from 1951–1953.

A&M had been described in a *Saturday Evening Post* story the previous spring as "the noisiest college in the USA." It certainly was this night after its only conference triumph of the year. The Farmers hadn't beaten Texas since 1939.

"Why is it," an Aggie-ex had asked the *Post* writer, "that everybody hates the school and we all love each other?" 🏈

1954

A Proud Tradition Continues, A Dubious One Ends

Bear Bryant made his mark at Texas A&M right off. He immediately earned a reputation as a tyrant, a label that would stay with him for many years, at his infamous training camp. Bryant left College Station with ninety-six players for the pre-season sessions at Junction, west of Austin. He returned with twenty-seven—the others had quit. The temperature was 110 degrees some days, Jack Pardee would remember. "It was an effort to survive," Pardee said. "Each player could tell his own story but mine was simply to make it to the next practice." After four years at College Station and twenty-three unbelievably successful years at his alma mater, Alabama, the Bear told *Time* magazine, "I don't know if what I did was good or bad. I will never know. It was just the only thing I could have done—at that time, knowing what I knew then. I wouldn't do it now because I know more than I knew then, more about resting players, letting them drink water, more about other ways to lead them. They had to put up with my stupidity. I believe if I'd been one of those players, I'd have quit, too."

Those who walked out of the training camp missed a season of futility. Georgia was the Aggies' lone victim in ten games. Texas also was struggling under Ed Price and recorded a losing season, but the Steers beat the Aggies 22–13, clinching it with a field goal with 1:08 left. The Memorial Stadium tradition lived on.

In attendance at the 1954 meeting was "Mr. A&M." P. L. Downs, Jr., had come into contact with Aggie football when he started school there in 1902. He was said to eat, sleep, and dream A&M evermore. An ex-

Bear Bryant, 1954: "I don't think there is any dissension on this team, but if there is I'm going to cause it."

member of A&M's board of directors, he was now the college's official greeter. The *American* said of Downs, "He dies a thousand deaths when the Aggies lose, but the Aggies never lose. Something happened to cause them to be outscored. He goes sleepless when the Aggies are outscored, sleeps soundly when they win. 'One of the regrets of my life,' he says, 'was when I could not buy a home on the campus of A&M.' He bought one within a stone's throw and grows maroon and white radishes in his garden. He prays at night: 'Lord, take care of the Aggies tonight. I'll take over in the morning.'"

Max Bickler was at the game, too. Bickler had seen every Texas-A&M contest ever staged, all sixty-one of them, and had officiated at four.

But one fellow, by the name of Duke Washington, had never been to an A&M-Texas game. He no doubt never saw one in his life, but when "the Duke" and his Washington State teammates played Texas back in October, he made history. The first black to play in Memorial Stadium, Washington received a thundering ovation from the crowd of 30,000 when he blazed seventy-three yards for a touchdown. The applause might have been somewhat softer had Texas not been winning, 40–14.

1955

The Bear Learns To Be Honest

Of the dozens of remarkable personalities involved in the UT-A&M rivalry, Bear Bryant may have been the most remarkable. He arrived at Texas A&M in 1954 from the University of Kentucky; in his eight years there, the Wildcats took their only Southeast Conference title. After restoring A&M to power in four years, he returned to Alabama and established a dynasty. Going into the 1981 season, Bryant's teams had recorded 306 victories (8 short of the record set by Pop Warner at Chicago University and the University of the Pacific) against 79 losses and 16 ties.

Bryant's second year at College Station started badly when the school was placed on probation for recruiting violations. The Bear acknowledges now that the violations took place, but insists that they were standard practice. Wealthy alumni gave players money, cars, and jobs. "All the other schools were doing it, so we did it, too," he said years later. "I was real bitter about it at the time—I cried all the way home from the meeting

where they put us on probation—but looking back, it may have been the best thing that ever happened to me. After that, I always lived by the letter of the law, never won a game anything but the honest way."

The Farmers were honestly undefeated in conference play and had even beaten eventual champ TCU, which had All-America Jim Swink. Rumors got the best of the rivalry this year, as stories circulated that Texas students had branded the latest Reveille, A&M's mascot, and started the A&M bonfire; neither actually happened. Highly coveted senior privileges were offered annually to any cadet who could steal Texas' cannon, "Smokey," but that didn't come off in 1955 either.

What did happen? Max Bickler missed his first game ever. And A&M missed its chance at the SWC title when Texas won, 21–6, at College Station.

1956

"There Is No Jinx"

Bryant's third team at A&M went into Memorial Stadium on November 29 with the best shot at breaking the jinx that any Aggie

"Big Bertha," the world's largest drum, was constructed for the University of Chicago in 1922. Atomic bomb research at Chicago's stadium contaminated the 500-pound, 8-foot high instrument. Texas paid Chicago $1 for the drum in 1955; the price included decontamination.

Fullback Jack Pardee survived the Junction training camp to earn All-America honors in 1956.

squad had had since the 1940 Farmers were upset 7–0. For the first time ever, the Aggies were on the roof in the league standings while the Longhorns occupied the basement. The Aggies were undefeated, and only once tied (by the University of Houston), because Bryant had worked his players mercilessly. At one point in the season, All-Southwest Conference running back John David Crow went into the dressing room after an Aggie practice, pulled off his sweat-soaked uniform, and sat on a chair in the shower. As Crow relaxed, Bryant called the team out for more practice. Crow struggled onto the field and fainted in the heat.

Teenage Rebel, all about "her first boyfriend, drag races, and rock 'n' roll," was showing at Austin's Paramount Theater Thanksgiving week. On Monday, bandleader Tommy Dorsey was found dead in his Connecticut home. In Austin, the Bear wasn't about to get sentimental over the Memorial Stadium jinx. "I don't think there is any such thing as a jinx," he said. And there wasn't, at least that Thanksgiving, as the Aggies ended Texas' worst season ever with a 34–21 haymaker. Excited cadets carried their heroes off the field, then returned to give Memorial's goal posts a serious rocking, but they couldn't bring them down.

Ed Price strolled solemnly off the field after his last game as Texas football coach. His 1–9 mark for the year (the only win was 7–6 over Tulane) was blamed partly on Texas' newly toughened academic standards. Bryant, meanwhile, finished his first undefeated year by going 9–0–1. A&M was still on probation, however, so TCU slipped into the Cotton Bowl for the second straight year, against Syracuse. The SWC concluded its first perfect season—each team lost only to teams ranked above it. A&M was champ at 6–0, TCU second with 5–1, Baylor third at 4–2, and so on. At the bottom was Texas, 0–6. ⬤

Aggie fish give a holler during freshman week, 1956.

1957

A Heisman for A&M

After Texas' poor showing in 1956, President Logan Wilson, who had raised scholastic standards, was hanged in effigy once. Outgoing coach Ed Price was hanged in effigy thrice. "I guess," Dr. Wilson said, "the only job more demanding than the president's is the football coach's." Stepping into that demanding position in 1957 was an Oklahoma graduate named Darrell Royal. An Austin newspaper commented, "There are two games, A&M and OU, that Royal cannot afford to lose consistently if he wants to remain the Texas coach."

The Texas job was Royal's seventh since he left Oklahoma in 1950. He had created a 17–13 win-loss mark at Mississippi State and the University of Washington, and was recommended to Texas officials by Bobby Dodd of Georgia Tech and Duffy Daugherty of Michigan State. He arrived a year after UT's academic standards had been toughened; Texas became the first state school in the U.S. to require entrance exams of all students. Its scholastic requirements were now higher than Rice's but, still, lower than Texas A&M's.

Royal's meeting with Bear Bryant on Thanksgiving was the only time the two would ever be across a field from each other. Bryant told *Life* magazine that year, "A boy's got to want to play awful bad to play here." John David Crow wanted to play badly enough that he won the Heisman trophy. As Texas and A&M went to war against each other, a bowl game was a certainty for the winner. A&M had beaten its first eight foes and was No. 1 in the nation before being upset 7–6 by Rice. Texas then edged the Farmers, 9–7, and went to the Sugar Bowl, where Mississippi romped, 39–7. A&M took the Gator Bowl invitation that Texas didn't want, and lost to Tennessee, 3–0. 🏈

1958

"Shovel-Shovers" Shut Out

Texas 27, Texas A&M 0.
Don Allen, injured Texas fullback: "I'd

Bear Bryant on the awarding of the 1957 Heisman Trophy: "If John David doesn't get it, they ought to quit giving it." Crow, All-Southwest Conference halfback at Aggieland in 1956 and 1957, also achieved All-America status in 1957.

sure rather sit on the bench and beat A&M than play and lose."

Longhorn co-captain Arlis Parkhurst: "Beating Oklahoma [15–14] and A&M in the same year sure makes it good."

Texas tackle Bill Stolhandske: "They didn't stand a chance from the kickoff. We were really up for them. I guess that just goes with being a Longhorn." Stolhandske held the game ball in his locker.

Texas coach Darrell Royal: "We haven't been contacted [by bowls]. Frankly, we don't care about going. We've had ten hard games and our season is over." The 'Horns finished at 7–3, all three defeats coming in SWC play.

Aggies, called a "pre-totemic tribe of shovel-shovers" by *Texan* editor Robb Burlage, had reverted to their old misdirected tricks by trying to light Texas' bonfire a little

early—it didn't work. On the same night, cadets were caught tearing down the winner of the beat-the-Aggies sign contest.

At the game, played in rainy 41-degree weather, the original manuscript of "The Eyes of Texas" (penned on laundry paper in 1903) was presented to Texas at halftime by Dr. James L. Johnson of Amarillo. Also, the Santa Rita oil well was memorialized. The flow of income that the Santa Rita had initiated on May 28, 1923, eventually totaled $550 million, two-thirds of which went to Texas, one-third to A&M. Bear Bryant was gone. He had returned to Alabama after the 1957 season and his replacement was Iowa State's Jim Myers. Against Texas, Myers's Aggies couldn't stop Royal's split-T offense, while the 'Horns stopped five serious A&M threats to rack up the big shutout. 🏈

Bear Bryant answered the call of his alma mater and left A&M for Alabama after the 1957 season.

Program.

The Texas Longhorn Band memorialized Santa Rita's fueling of the University fortune during half-time festivities, 1958.

1959

It Could Have Made the Season

Lou Maysel, *American-Statesman* sports editor, made note of the growing strength of the Southwest Conference and the effect it had on its own members' efforts to achieve perfect seasons. He stated in a column:

All teams here in the SWC are vulnerable to the upset because of the fierceness of the rivalry, but Texas and A&M are the two schools that have the toughest time of getting through without being bumped off. . . . All of the SWC teams take special delight in whipping the big state school, Texas, and most of them have a special antipathy for the Aggies. Since the SWC finally went to a complete round-robin in football in 1934, the first year Arkansas

and Texas A&M played all the other league members, the SWC has had only seven champs that have gone through all six games without defeat or tie. This tosses out the '43 Texas team which licked the five other wartime members and had a tremendous manpower edge, not of its own making, over the rest. The seven to go 6–0 for the SWC campaign were the '35 SMU, '38 TCU, '39 A&M, '49 Rice, '50 Texas, '52 Texas and '56 A&M teams. The former three are generally regarded as super teams and the latter four as extraordinary ones, and yet none of them was able to really coast on through.

The 1959 season was no different from most SWC years, as no SWC team went undefeated in league play. Don Meredith was stirring excitement at SMU with his amazing passing and "hair-breadth style of play," TCU was solid and strong. It was Texas that threatened to tie TCU for the crown going into the A&M game. The Aggies led Texas 10–0 at

halftime, then Texas came back to lead by four points in the third quarter. The passing of Charley Milstead gave A&M the edge again at 17–14, but Texas rolled right back down the green of Kyle Field to win 20–17. A&M thus lost its last chance to win a conference game in 1959, and it was a chance that would have redeemed the entire season. Co-champ Texas lost to Syracuse in the Cotton Bowl, 23–7. 🏈

Contestants in UT's 1958 Aggie Sign Contest portray cadets being ironed, booted, and insulted in various languages.

1960

Vacant Stares

"You may ask, who does go to Aggieland? Not many, good sport, not many," proposed Texas' student magazine, the *Texas Ranger*, in its November 1960 Aggie issue. "Each year the enrollment drops, each year the Five Thousand Fanatical Farmers find it harder to keep out the women ('If the Corps wanted yew to have wimmen, they'd a-issued yew wimmen!') and each year the poor Aggies sink deeper into a pool of nothingness, closer to extinction. One possible solution is to let females in; however, this would cause a number of troubles. Can you imagine how warped a poor kid would be if both his father *and* his mother were Aggies?"

Before the A&M game, a doleful Darrell Royal told reporters, "I'm flat scared to death." During his tenure at Texas, Royal would become known for his miserable outlook immediately preceding each huge Texas victory, but with the 1960 Aggies, his fear was justified. Texas' yearbook, the *Cactus*, described the situation: "The Longhorns put everything on the line in their annual Thanksgiving Day battle with arch rival Texas A&M. Not only a successful season, but also a bid to the Bluebonnet Bowl hung in the balance. The Steers (4–2 in SWC play with the addition this year of Texas Tech to the league) showed early that they meant to have this one. On the first play from scrimmage, an Aggie jump pass was batted into the air and James Saxton came down with the ball on the Farmers' 32. Six plays later, Saxton capped the drive as he slashed through a gaping hole at left tackle to score from the 3." Texas led 21–0 at the half. A&M assistant coach Bobby Drake Keith, who had spent the first thirty minutes of the game in the press box on the phone to the bench, came into the Aggie locker room at intermission and said to the players, "Any of you who think you did your job, look me in the eye." None of them did. A&M did earn two second-half touchdowns, but UT's first-half dominance held up.

Charley Milstead took All-Southwest Conference honors at the A&M quarterback position in 1958.

James Saxton (1961 All-America) eludes A&M defenders en route to a winning-margin touchdown in the 1960 game in Austin.

Seniors form an honor guard for the 1957 Aggie team at Kyle Field, as Texas players watch.

The A&M-UT student council attempted to coordinate activities surrounding the annual clash.

Program.

T. K. Kirkpatrick (Class of '54)
used his Reagan, Texas, barn
to prove he's an Aggie for life.

Coach Jim Myers addresses Aggies at yell practice, as yell leader Ted Lowe stands by.

Head yell leader, Bill Dorsey, extracts spirit from the cadet corps.

THE

1960's

1961

Saxton Triumphant

Texas was having no problems on its way to Kyle Field in 1961. Its foes met similar fates week after week, 28–3, 42–14, 41–8, 28–7, 33–7, 34–7, 27–0, 33–7. The Longhorns were riding atop the national polls after thumping their first eight foes (making twelve straight victories over 1960-61), with only a weak TCU and a weaker A&M left to play. In 1898 and 1906 Texas had preserved spotless records by beating the Frogs, but on the four occasions since on which it had reached the TCU game without a loss, it was beaten. Before the 1961 game at Memorial Stadium, TCU coach Abe Martin surveyed his 2–5–1 team's chances and stated, "If I were in Darrell Royal's shoes, I wouldn't be worried." But Royal said, "I'm as nervous as a pig in a packing plant."

On an overcast November Saturday, Texas intercepted Sonny Gibbs's pass on the first play of the game. All-America running back James Saxton corralled a Mike Cotten pass and galloped forty-five yards to the TCU ten. Donnie Smith tackled him, and as Saxton rolled over on the ground, he was hit late by TCU tackle Bobby Plummer. The Texas star was knocked out cold and only on his second try was he able to walk off the field. The rest of the Texas offense moved the ball to the one-yard line, where the Frog defense held on fourth down. Later in the half, TCU had the ball at the fifty-yard line. *Sports Illustrated*'s staff Frog, Dan Jenkins, described the next play: "Sonny Gibbs, who looks a bit like the state capitol in shoulder pads, called a pass." And it was some pass—a fifty-yard gainer on a fleaflicker to Buddy Iles, giving the twenty-four-point underdogs a 6–0 lead over the nation's top team. Texas blocked the point-after kick, but TCU proceeded to stop Texas at the Frogs' three, twenty-one, and twenty-seven to protect the fragile lead. Saxton returned to play in the third quarter and was knocked out again. In the fourth period, back for more, he completed his eighty-five-yard day (on seventeen carries) by leading Texas from its own thirty-eight to TCU's eight. On fourth down, a wall of purple smothered quarterback Cotten, and Texas' fifty-yards-and-a-cloud-of-dust offense was shut out. After the astounding 6–0 upset, the 6'7"

UT fans had plenty to cheer about in 1961; despite a 6–0 upset by TCU, the Longhorns went on to a 12–7 victory over Mississippi in the Cotton Bowl.

Gibbs and tackle Plummer met Saxton at midfield to apologize. Saxton said, "There was nothing dirty about it, but you guys sure do hit hard." Plummer said later, "I was trying to miss him." In another historic game the same day, Notre Dame was awarded an extra play and kicked a field goal after time ran out to take a controversial 17–15 victory over Syracuse.

Only the Aggies remained on the Longhorns' schedule. Royal looked at it this way: "It's no disgrace to get knocked down as long as you get back up." On their home field, the Farmers made a goal-line stand in the second quarter to limit Texas to a 6–0 lead at the half on two field goals. But then *Sports Illustrated* coverboy Saxton, a native of College Station, threw his first pass of the season, and it went forty-six yards for a touchdown. Texas combined the running of Saxton, who claimed to be able to catch a half-grown jackrabbit, with the passing of Cotten to lift itself to a 25–0 victory and a co-championship with Arkansas. The Steers, then ranked No. 3, outlasted Mississippi, 12–7, in the Cotton Bowl. 🏈

1962

Bestest 13, Restest 3

"Maybe the trouble with A&M isn't the lack of women. Maybe it's the lack of men." The *Texas Ranger* annually poked fun at the Aggies. "Believe it or not, there are things to do at A&M College. . . . First off, there's the Aggie bonfire and yell practice. . . . Aggies have been practicing the same yells since 1876, or calling it practicing, and they have learned them pretty well. They will probably do some of the everpopular ones like 'Gig 'em' and 'A-G-G-I-E-S' and if the spirit moves them far enough they may become overly fervent and begin tossing toilet paper (Aggie confetti) gaily about. The Aggie bonfire and yell practice are really something to see, if you haven't been to a good old-fashioned pagan ritual and fire dance lately."

Jim Myers wasn't A&M's coach anymore. He had been dismissed before the 1961 meeting with Texas because of a fourth-place finish in the league that year. He was replaced

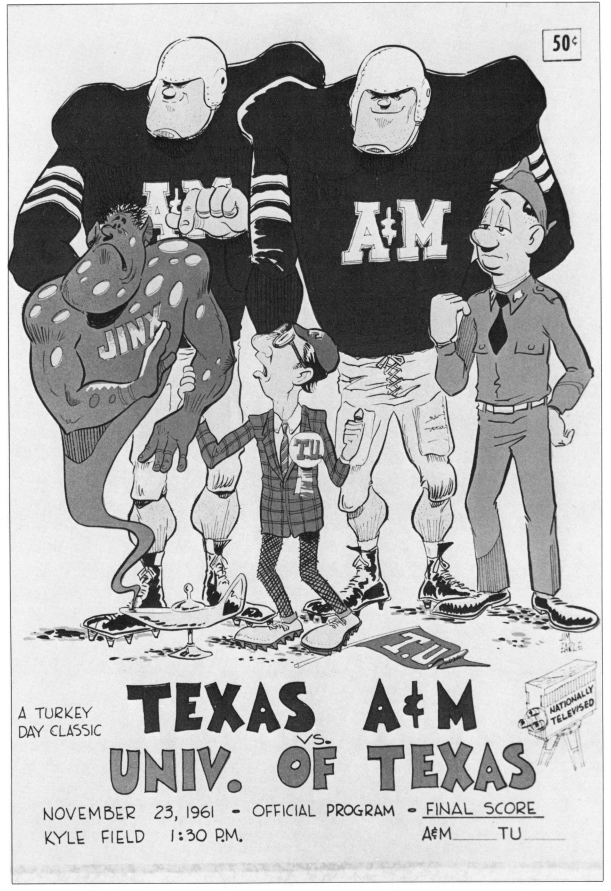

A TURKEY DAY CLASSIC

TEXAS A&M
vs.
UNIV. OF TEXAS

NOVEMBER 23, 1961 · OFFICIAL PROGRAM · <u>FINAL SCORE</u>
KYLE FIELD 1:30 P.M.   A&M_____ TU_____

50¢

NATIONALLY TELEVISED

When the smoke cleared, the blanks at the bottom of the 1961 program cover were filled with A&M 0, UT 25.

by Hank Foldberg. UT, meanwhile, with All-America guard John Treadwell, had dodged defeat through nine games, although their record contained a 14–14 deadlock with longtime nemesis Rice that lost the 'Horns' No. 1 ranking. The undefeated team was Texas' first since 1923, and it earned Texas its first outright SWC title since 1952. The Farmers had been known to use fifty-three different offensive formations, but most teams figured them out and gave A&M a 3–4 SWC mark, for a fourth-place finish.

Texas fan and humorist Cactus Pryor coined some pre-game poetry: "Texas, Texas, we're the bestest/Aggies play like Billie Sol Estes." On what the *Austin American-Statesman* called "two holidays rolled into one," the Aggies led 3–0 on national television for the first three quarters of the Thanksgiving Day clash. But Texas won the restest on 13 unanswered final period points. They went on to the Cotton Bowl, but lost to LSU, 13–0.

Hank Foldberg, a former West Point All-America and Aggie head coach from 1962 to 1964, called the 1963 loss to UT "the greatest injustice on a group of young fellows I've ever seen."

Farmer quarterback Jim Keller makes a dash for daylight during the 1962 game against Houston.

Hank Foldberg, in his first full year as Aggie head coach, stacks up the advantages on his side, 1962.

Aggie quarterback Jim Keller, 1962.

The man of the hour in UT's come-from-behind victory over the Aggies in 1963, Emmett "Duke" Carlisle.

1963

"The Greatest Injustice"

It was a year of tragedy, of progress, and of an incredible game. Overshadowing everything else, President John F. Kennedy was gunned down six days before the game and on the very day he was scheduled to visit Austin. Texas and Texas A&M were two of four Southwest Conference schools to open their athletics to blacks, and women were admitted to A&M. Texas officials complained about A&M's football field, and some Aggies kid-

naped Bevo VII. And in the last two minutes of the game itself, A&M first threw away a victory and then had it stolen from them.

Kennedy's death in Dallas on Friday, November 22, threw a cloak of gloom over the nation's athletics just as it did over other aspects of American life. Many college football games, including two in the SWC, were postponed from the following day. By November 28, the day of the UT-A&M clash, Texas' own Lyndon Johnson had been president for six days.

On a Wednesday two weeks before, dormitory residents at A&M had been awakened by cries of "We have Bevo!" The kidnaping of Texas' steer was the fifth such theft of an op-

ponent's mascot that season by the Aggies. The perpetrators initially planned to cut off Bevo's fifty-four inch horns but then decided just to keep him until the game. Under intense pressure from officials of both schools, however, the cadets responsible allowed the steer to be found at a hiding place six miles south of College Station. Texas students responded by pouring chemicals (the Aggies suspected tea) on Kyle Field to kill the grass in the shape of the word *BEVO*. Crews for the television network broadcasting the game nationally dyed the area green but the dead grass, soaked by days of rain, came loose during the game, and a quagmire developed. Frank Erwin, a member of the Texas Board of Regents, protested vehemently at halftime, saying that "no university which makes any pretense at having a major athletic program would permit such conditions to exist."

All the emotional activity only served to increase the tension for the game itself. In honor of Kennedy, the Aggies canceled their bonfire—that was considered the greatest sacrifice A&M could make—and the team wore black armbands. Quarterback Jim Keller remembered Homer Norton's quote about showing up at the showdown, and pride ran strong. With the fourth quarter almost gone, the Longhorns, 9–0 and rated No. 1 in the nation, found themselves behind due to a fanatical effort by the Aggies, including an interception returned for a touchdown by Travis Reagan. Lucky Tommy Wade replaced Duke Carlisle at quarterback and began moving the Longhorns from their own twenty-one. On that final drive, A&M managed to intercept two Texas passes, but to no avail. John Brotherton grabbed the first, but on his run back tried to lateral the ball, fumbled it instead, and saw Texas recover. Then Jim Willenborg snared one in the end zone at the back line. He was ruled out of bounds over vehement Aggie protest and Texas retained possession. Carlisle returned to the field long enough to knife in from the one-yard line with 1:19 left, and give A&M an undeserved 15–13 loss, their seventh in ten games. After what Hank Foldberg called "the greatest injustice on a group of young fellows I've ever seen"—he didn't like the call on Willenborg at all—A&M president Earl Rudder declared the next Monday a school holiday. Texas spent a different holiday at the Cotton Bowl, where it sank Roger Staubach and his Navy mates, 28–6. 🏈

UT quarterback Tommy Wade's two intercepted passes didn't stop the 'Horns from defeating the Aggies 15–13, 1963.

1964

The Year Nobis Stopped Namath

Hank Foldberg writing Barry Goldwater: "I know just how you feel." That's how Cactus Pryor viewed the Aggie coach's situation. Foldberg was under fire for a season that included only one victory, that over SMU. The *Bryan Daily Eagle* reported that Bud Wilkinson, head coach and athletic director at Oklahoma University, had visited A&M about the job. Also reported to have been interviewed was Aggie alumnus Willie Zapalac, an assistant to Bear Bryant and Jim Myers at A&M and now an assistant to Darrell Royal in Austin.

Texan staffer Paul Burka opined in print that the A&M game no longer was a tradition but "just another game in which the mighty Longhorns rolled over their hapless opponents." The *Battalion* staff was infuriated and pointed out that A&M had won the league basketball and baseball championships in 1964. But to a great degree, Burka was right. Texas had won twenty-one games in the series since 1940, A&M only two. The University of Oklahoma had become Texas' foremost rival by virtue of the two teams' relative parity. Arkansas, too, was quickly becoming a favorite foe for Texas players and fans. And that fire was stoked on October 17 at Memorial Stadium when Texas, 4–0 for the year and trying to nurse a winning streak to sixteen games, shunned a tie and went for the winning two points after a late touchdown. It failed, and Arkansas, which would finish the year as champions at 10–0 and defeat Nebraska in Dallas on New Year's Day, escaped by a hair, 14–13.

Still, an Aggie was an Aggie, and Longhorn fans manifested their loyalty noisily, as they had at seventy previous A&M-Texas encounters. Texas had played Oklahoma only fifty-eight games prior to 1964, Baylor fifty-three times, and all its other foes fifty times or fewer. At Memorial, the mighty Longhorns rolled over their hapless opponent, 26–7, then faced Bear Bryant and his Crimson Tide in the Cotton Bowl. With the Steers ahead 21–17, quarterback Joe Namath led Alabama to the Texas one-yard line. From there, in three plays, not only did Namath fail to cross the goal, no Alabama lineman got across. That defensive stand, led by linebacker Tommy Nobis, turned the 21–17 lead into a victory.

Tommy Nobis, All-America linebacker for Texas, was later drafted by the Atlanta Falcons of the National Football League as their number one pick.

Aggie back, Jim Kaufman (with ball) *was a crucial element in Gene Stallings' "Texas Special" trick play, 1965.*

1965

The "Texas Special"

Evolution of the Aggie joke:

1937

One Aggie: "What was that explosion on the chicken farm?"

Second Aggie: "I fed the chickens some 'lay-or-bust' feed and one of them was a rooster."

1956

Two Aggies went to a rather bawdy carnival that once played near their trading post.

One of the sideshows featured a couple of nude babes playing badminton in a show called "Exercise of the Ancients." The Aggies watched, fascinated. Finally, one turned to the other and said, "Good show, huh?"

"Yeah, it's ok," answered the other, "but where in hell's the scoreboard?"

1962

Two men got on an elevator and as the door closed, one said to the other, "Say, you went to Harvard, didn't you?"

"Yes, I did," answered the other. "How could you tell?"

"Oh, I could tell by the nice clothes you have," said the first, "and the proud way you

carry yourself and by the educated look you have."

"Well, thank you," the second man said. "You went to A&M, didn't you?"

"Yes," replied the first, "how could you tell?"

"Well, it was easy. I saw your class ring when you reached up to pick your nose."

1965

House detective: "Are you entertaining a woman in your room?"

Aggie: "Just a minute, I'll ask her."

1979

The Aggies have purchased 300 septic tanks. As soon as they learn how to drive them they plan to attack the University of Texas.

Those are the nice ones. In 1965, The Aggie joke became somewhat official with the publication of *101 Aggie Jokes*, put together by one Aggie, the sister of an Aggie, and a graduate of TCU. There were 104 jokes in the book and the Frog blamed the other two for the miscount. Volumes 2 through 8 followed from 1965 through 1979, and the Aggie joke took its place in American humor. Most Aggies enjoyed them and poked fun at themselves, such as with the banner displayed at an A&M dormitory in 1978: "Beat the Hell Outta Open Date."

November 25, 1965, was no open date for the Aggies. In building a 17–0 first-half lead at Kyle, the Aggies used a Tea-Sipper joke, also known as the "Texas Special." Quarterback Harry Ledbetter took the snap and tossed a one-bounce lateral to Jim Kaufman. It looked like an incomplete pass to everybody but the Aggies. Kaufman stomped his foot in disgust, Ledbetter slammed fist into hand, and Dude McLean stopped in the middle of his pass route. Then McLean took off and Kaufman passed to him for a ninety-one yard touchdown. But Texas scored three touchdowns in the final half and had the last laugh, 21–17.

1966

The "Not So Special"

"There really is only one game a year and it is with the Aggies."

So much for the diminution of the rivalry. That was Longhorn wingback Jim Helms talking. Helms had scored two touchdowns in Texas' 1965 comeback, and his father, Jake, was A&M's freshman coach. Longhorn defensive tackle Diron Talbert phrased it this way: "The Bluebonnet Bowl would be great

1966 marked the debut of Reveille III, shown here looking over the official uniform of Reveille II.

All-Southwest Conference defensive tackle Diron Talbert played at UT from 1964 to 1966.

Chris Gilbert put UT ahead 7–0 on its first possession, and the 'Horns went on to defeat the Aggies 22–14, 1966. Gilbert was both an All-America and All-Southwest Conference selection in 1968.

but A&M is more important." Reveille III and Bevo IX both made their debut at the 1966 game. Reveilles I and II had been buried near the entrance to Kyle Field. "They are there," goes the Aggie explanation, "so they can see the scoreboard and know how the game is going."

The A&M coach, in his second year, was former Aggie star Gene Stallings. It was Stallings who had designed the "Texas Special" in 1965, and it was Stallings's "Texas Special No. 2" that helped the Aggies pull within a point of Texas in the first half of the 1966 battle at Memorial Stadium. Quarterback Bill Bradley and outstanding running back Chris Gilbert had put Texas ahead 7–0 on its first possession. Of the "Texas Special," conspirator Jim Kauffman had said, "We knew it wasn't good nor sound football, but when you're outpersonneled as we were, you've got to get any edge you can." The Farmers were again "outpersonneled," but the "Texas Special No. 2" wasn't nearly as unorthodox as its predecessor. Bob Long took the kickoff after Texas' score and faked a handoff to Lloyd Currington before heading six yards upfield and turning for the sideline. Long then pitched to Currington, who had been running laterally with him. Despite an injured thigh, Currington made tracks to Texas' twenty-three before being caught. The Aggies pushed into the end zone but were left a point shy when their kick sailed wide to the left. Just before the half, Texas succeeded on its only pass completion of the day, a sixty-one-yarder from Bradley to Tom Higgins for a score. A fumble and two interceptions aided Texas in building a 22–6 margin before A&M scored with a minute left for a 22–14 final. The 'Horns did, indeed, find the Bluebonnet Bowl "great," punching Mississippi 19–0.

1967

Jubilation Junction

College Station's mayor proposed that the name of the town be changed. After all, Texas A&M had recently been declared a university, and the old railroad station had been torn down. After learning of the mayor's wish, students at the University of Texas held a town-naming contest. The winning entry was Malfunction Junction. The mayor apparently decided College Station sounded rather good. By the end of the 1967 football season, however, Jubilation Junction would be appropriate.

You wouldn't have bet on it in October. Bumper stickers around town declared "The Aggies Are Back," but they began with losses to SMU, Purdue, LSU, and Florida State. Like-

During the 1968 game Bill Bradley (with ball) *haunted Aggie quarterback Edd Hargett, intercepting four passes.*

Coach Gene Stallings and quarterback Edd Hargett (1968 All-Southwest Conference) show their Cotton Bowl game plan, 1968.

wise, Texas' start was a slow one, including season-opening losses to Southern California and Texas Tech. Then both schools began racking up league victories and appeared to be on a collision course for the title. However, the 'Horns tripped over TCU, and A&M kicked them as they fell. A Texas victory over the Aggies would have split the crown between Tech, A&M, and Texas, but the Longhorns came away from Kyle Field three points shy, 10–7. As in the previous fifty-one years of Southwest Conference in-fighting, two league losses spelled doom. It was an

eighty-yard bomb from Edd Hargett to Bob Long that elevated the Aggies past Texas and into the Cotton Bowl, ending a ten-year winning streak by the Teasippers in the series. It was Darrell Royal's first loss to A&M in his ten years as Texas coach. After the Farmers upset Alabama 20–16 on January 1, 1968, Bear Bryant helped carry his former protégé, Stallings, from the field.

Texas finished at 6–4 for the third straight year. But, as Chris Gilbert said, "You can't call a 6–4 season a winning one." Goodness, no. 🏈

1968

Bradley the Burglar

The Battalion printed a letter it claimed it had received:

> We are two University of Texas coeds. My roommate is 6'2" tall and weighs 86 pounds. She is slightly bow-legged, has hairy legs and has a case of halitosis (that's bad breath for you

His passing game thwarted, Edd Hargett scrambles for an Aggie gain against the Longhorns, 1968.

Aggies who don't understand). I am a very well-rounded person, being 5' tall and weighing 300 pounds. I have a slight case of acne, but am getting it cleared up. I have buck teeth, a big nose and a flat hairy chest. Both of us are nice girls, just what all you Aggies want. We write our mothers every day, make our own clothes and the frat rats here at t.u. love us. If any of you Aggies would like to chance for a date for the Turkey Day game, just write. Lynn Lizard and Pattie Pig.

Two *Battalion* staffers responded, in part: "Unfortunately, we both have dates for the Turkey Day game already, but just can't stand the thought of somebody else kissing you when the Aggies score. If we can't have you, *nobody* can."

Possibly the most admirable tradition among "the proudest squares," as the Aggies were called in a *Sports Illustrated* report, has been their privilege of getting a kiss from their dates whenever the football team scores. Aggies didn't win many kisses in 1968. The Farmers were expected to cop the SWC title, but they won only two conference games. Texas, meanwhile, was entering a five-year period in which it would lose only six games, despite starting off the 1968 campaign with an 0–1–1 mark. The Longhorns won seven straight after that start, going into the Aggie game. "To a

smoker it's a Kent; to a UT football player it's closing out the regular season of his senior year against Texas A&M in Memorial Stadium," reported an Austin newspaper. A&M's Edd Hargett came into the televised battle having thrown 176 straight passes without an interception. But he coughed up 5 against Texas, 4 to the versatile Bill Bradley, and when the smoke cleared, the Aggies found themselves kissed off, 35–14. Texas, as SWC co-champ with Arkansas, went on to burn Tennessee in the Cotton Bowl, 36–13.

1969

The Incredible Season

Texas had three tough games in 1969; A&M wasn't one of them. By the time the Steers crunched the Ags 49–12 on a wet November day, they were unbeaten through nine games of one of the most astonishingly successful seasons in the 100-year history of college football. The Sooners were Texas' fourth opponent. Oklahoma, where Darrell Royal had played four years against Texas, jumped out to a 14–0 lead in a battle of undefeated teams. But quarterback James Street and running back Jim Bertelsen led the Steers back to a 27–17 victory.

Four more conference foes lined up to take their lumps before the Aggies tried,

and failed, to end Texas' rush in the last game played on Kyle Field grass. "The Game of the Century," "The Big Shootout," or just the most important SWC game since the 1935 SMU-TCU gangfight—it was labeled all these and more—came nine days later. Texas' game with Arkansas had been moved to the end of the season to accommodate the television producers: it was the Texas Longhorns, No. 1 in the nation, 9–0 for the year, and undefeated in their last eighteen games, versus the Arkansas Razorbacks, No. 2 in the nation, 9–0 for the year, and undefeated in their last fifteen games. The setting was Razorback Stadium, Fayetteville, Arkansas, where the rabid fans call hogs with a shrillness and unity of purpose that make any Texan shiver. They had a lot to holler about as their heroes played their "game of a lifetime," burying Texas 14–0 through three quarters on a gray winter afternoon. But, in the fourth period, the overflow crowd (which included President Richard Nixon) felt a chill. James "Slick" Street provided it when he ran, on second-and-nine, forty-two yards for a touchdown. Texas successfully tried for two points on the PAT, and Arkansas' lead was trimmed to 14–8.

Arkansas soon had its chance from Texas' seven, but a pass into the end zone was intercepted. Still, as the gloom of dusk descended upon unlighted Razorback Stadium, the day looked especially dark for

1969 marked Kyle Field's last season with a natural grass field.

President Richard Nixon (standing at right) *applauds as Darrell Royal and the 'Horns receive the MacArthur Bowl for National College Football Supremacy. Standing behind Royal* (from left) *are Texas tri-captains James Street, Ted Koy, and Glenn Haskell.*

UT quarterback James Street of the 1969 national championship team.

Two good reasons for Texas' success in 1969, All-Southwest Conference players Jim Bertelsen (35) and Steve Worster (30).

Randy Peschel practices for what James Street called "only the greatest catch in the history of football" in UT's defeat of Arkansas in the Big Shoot Out.

Texas. With less than five minutes remaining in the game, the 'Horns found themselves bottled up in their own territory and facing a fourth down. On Royal's order, Street reared back and heaved the football as far as he could. Forty-four yards downfield, tight end Randy Peschel made what Street called "only the greatest catch in the history of football." Off balance, Peschel brought it down out of the darkness from between two defenders. Bertelsen tied the score at 3:58 with a touchdown run, and Happy Feller's

kick provided the winning margin. Bill Montgomery moved the Hogs to Texas' thirty-nine, but a Tom Campbell interception ended the game.

Texas was not through working miracles. With the three surviving members of the Four Horsemen looking on in the Cotton Bowl, January 1, 1970, Ara Parseghian's Fighting Irish of Notre Dame followed the pattern—they led Texas late in the fourth quarter, 17–14. Street, facing his second fourth down in two minutes, sent a pass in

the direction of receiver Cotten Speyrer. The throw was low and Speyrer dived, coming up with a phenomenal catch for a first down with 2:26 remaining. Three plays later, Billy Dale crossed the goal for a 21–17 victory in what *Sports Illustrated*'s Dan Jenkins called "as courageous a game as any two schools played throughout the whole of the century." It was the second such game for Texas in a month's time.

Longhorn halfback Billy Dale hurdles for a gain of 7 yards in the 1969 A&M game.

1970

Softening Them Up for the Irish

The folks over at tea-sippers university ("little *t*, little *u*, periods optional") had always kidded the Aggies about their military-strict, womanless education. But goodness, how things were changing on the old gray campus by the 1970s. Females were attending A&M in quickly increasing numbers, and President Earl Rudder also had made cadet corps service noncompulsory in 1965, so by now civvies were common on campus, even if the hippies familiar to UT and other American colleges were in extremely small numbers at A&M. Although women were in the cadet corps, and known as Waggies, the Texas Aggie Band remained a male bastion.

The Battalion asked the inevitable question: "Should women be allowed to be yell leaders?" One male senior snapped, "No! Women belong in the stands as dates." Even a female responded, "No. . . . The very idea is nauseating. Women should not try to wreck the traditions of their school." A graduate student, male, sneered, "No, they can't yell loud enough to tell a fable." And besides, what would women yell leaders squeeze while the men are holding their genitals to "help bear the pain" for the football players?

University of Texas football fans continued to expect magic acts in 1970, and the Long-horns pleased them in the third game. The Steers required—and got—a forty-five-yard touchdown pass twelve seconds before the end to beat UCLA 20–17. One week later, Texas turned the Sooner players as red as their Oklahoma jerseys, 41–9. Only Baylor played Texas close (21–14). As in the year

before, the Aggies were but a sparring partner before the Big Shootout II. In a game dedicated to prisoners of war and those unaccounted for in Vietnam, the Aggies were missing in action. A&M left the ball on the artificial surface of Memorial Stadium six times and couldn't beat the thirty-three-point spread gamblers had posted. Texas suffered injuries in the 52–14 romp, however, and with Arkansas next in line, Darrell Royal pleaded, "If anybody knows Oral Roberts on a first-name basis, let's get him down here."

In the Big Mismatch December 5 in Austin, Texas beat Arkansas 42–7 for its thirtieth straight victory. But guess who was back in Dallas for the Revenge Bowl. The SWC champs found themselves flat out of miracles on January 1. Notre Dame's 24–11 triumph ended the streak, but not the sovereignty. Arkansas, which certainly deserved a bowl spot for its 9–2 performance, was left at home.

Cotton Speyrer, a hero in UT's 1970 defeat of Notre Dame in the Cotton Bowl, was All-Southwest Conference in 1969, and All-America in both 1969 and 1970.

The Aggie Band in formation, 1961. Though women have been admitted to the corps of cadets, the band still remains all-male.

The Longhorn Band marches in the inaugural parade for President John F. Kennedy, 1961. The Band gave a repeat performance in 1964 for President Lyndon B. Johnson's inauguration.

A meeting of great football minds, UT's Darrell Royal and A&M's Gene Stallings.

Aggie yell leaders and crowd participation urge the team to "saw 'Varsity horns off."

The Aggies score.

Travis Reagan scrambles for an Aggie gain.

1970's

1971

Spelling Lessons

The traditional bonfires met different fates at A&M and Texas in 1971. At Aggieland, the pre-Thanksgiving blaze had been canceled only once, in 1963, in all the years since it began as a joke when two cadets lit a trash pile in 1909. And in 1971, an enormous, well-planned effort was required to build, with the help of cranes, "the world's largest bonfire." Students in Austin, meanwhile, showed little interest in a bonfire, so for that and other reasons Texas' fire never burned. Year after year, the Aggies worked for days building their spirit spire, and then usually lost the game. Texas proved they could win without flames.

A&M's football team rebounded from five straight losses to a 5–5 posture by Thanksgiving. Liberty Bowl officials had extended an invitation to Aggie coach Gene Stallings if his boys could beat Texas. But the Longhorns, whom one student group wanted to rename the Armadillos, won 34–14, clinching for themselves a fourth straight SWC title and Cotton Bowl excursion. "I think," Stallings said after the game and while A&M officials were considering his fate, "they'll tell me I can coach here another year." He was fired.

"The Game of the Century" this year wasn't in the SWC, but the Big 8. When No. 1–ranked Nebraska scored late in the fourth quarter to beat No. 2–ranked Oklahoma 35–31 for the league crown and national championship, it climaxed a pulse-pounding play-off equal to the 1969 Texas-Arkansas game in almost every way. This year's Longhorns knew they faced trouble in Penn State, whose fans came to Dallas on January 1 with this cheer: "Give me a *T*, give me an *E*, give me an *X*, give me an *A*, give me an *S*, what's that spell? *SHIT!*" The Penn State football team was about as rough as its rooters, and buried Texas 30–6.

1972

The SWC's Winningest "Fraud"

"They're aggressive as hell and they're Aggies. They don't like Texas and I don't like them. I think I'm the only ex-Aggie who doesn't." Willie Zapalac, A&M '46, was now offensive line coach at the University of Texas. Emory Bellard, who as a Texas backfield coach had developed the wishbone offense that catapulted Texas ahead of the rest of the nation's football schools in the late 1960s, was A&M's rookie head coach in 1972. Donnie Wigginton, who had quarterbacked the Longhorns in their runaway victory at Kyle Field in 1971, was now Bellard's assistant. Darrell Royal stayed right where he was as Texas' head coach and marked up eight victories in his first nine games.

Royal endured an anxious week prior to the season finale against A&M in Memorial Stadium. *Meat on the Hoof*, a book by a former Texas player who was critical of the Texas brand of football, and an Associated Press series on black players had both just been released. In that week, Royal was branded "a racist, a hobnob to the governor and a fraud." He balanced his worries with a 38–3 hatchet job on the Aggies, making him the winningest coach in Southwest Conference history at eighty-seven victories in sixteen years, surpassing the record Rice's Jess Neely set in twenty-seven years.

Twenty-five Aggies did a lot of sweating in that week before the game, too. Divided into

UT quarterback Mike Rowan looks to unleash a pass before he is dumped in the 1972 A&M game.

UT's All-America and All-Southwest Conference tackle Jerry Sisemore, 1971–1972.

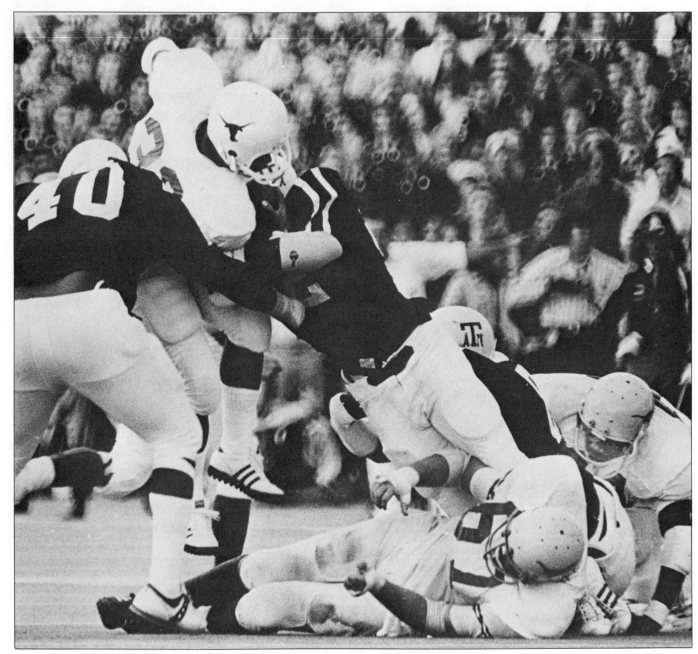

Linebacker John McCrumbly lifts UT's Lonnie Bennett off his feet, 1973.

two-man teams, they carried banners from College Station to Austin on foot in the "Walton Hall Fightin' Texas Aggie 'Beat Hell Outta t.u.' Marathon." Once in Austin, the Aggie runners circled Memorial Stadium, then sprinted to Eastwoods Park for yell practice.

Nebraska fans at their season-ending Oklahoma game in Lincoln, which the 'Huskers won 17–14, held up signs to the effect that Alabama was playing in the Chicken Bowl. Alabama players had voted to play Texas in the Cotton Bowl rather than face tough Nebraska. Texas proved tough enough, winning 17–13. ⬤

1973

The Hidden Center Play

The Aggies defeated Texas virtually every Thanksgiving week. In 1961, it was A&M 1,442, Texas 1,430, in rifle shooting. 1967, in addition to the football victory: A&M 14, Texas 10, in water polo, extending the Aggies' watery winning streak over the Longhorns to thirty-five years. 1973: A&M 33, Texas 18, in wrestling. But after the last three decades of

playing Texas, the Aggies had to admit that football was one game the Tea-Sippers knew how to play. That was a fact most of Texas' opponents knew so well. Of the nineteen schools that Texas had played at least four times in history and that were still playing major college ball, only four had winning records against Texas—Nebraska, Notre Dame, Southern Cal, and Vanderbilt. Among the football powers who learned that playing Texas probably would damage their win-loss records were Alabama, Louisiana State, Arkansas, Missouri, Auburn, and Oklahoma.

The 1973 edition of the Longhorns met

the Aggies with visions of a sixth straight Cotton Bowl and a fifth straight unshared SWC title. The Aggies did nothing to spoil the dream. Instead, the Farmers helped their foe to its nineteenth conference victory in its last nineteen games. As time was running out in the first half and A&M moved into Texas territory at Kyle Field, the Aggies were trailing 21–7 and had no time-outs remaining. They drove to the five, then were penalized back to the twenty. With eight seconds left, center Ricky Seeker ran off the field thinking there would be a field goal attempt. Wrong, Ricky! The Aggies broke the huddle, but there was no one to center the ball and time ran out.

Texas ran up 42 points to A&M's 13 and went to the Cotton Bowl (ho-hum), where Nebraska dealt them a 19–3 setback.

1974

Home, and Happy, for the Holidays

"Point spreads don't mean a thing. A&M and Texas—it's the same old bloodbath. It's just a matter of who hates who the most. It doesn't matter who plays who where." It might sound like a challenge from the rivalry of the 1930s, but it was Texas placekicker Billy Schott sizing up the 1974 battle against an A&M team ranked No. 9 in the nation with an 8–2 mark, its best in eighteen years. Still, No. 17-rated Texas was an eight-point favorite in the day-after-Thanksgiving game at Memorial Stadium. "I guess that's because we're playing here," said one Texas team member. But a Texas freshman named Earl Campbell stated, "That still doesn't win the game. That's all I've got to say about it." Darrell Royal, of course, ignored his school's 23–1–1 success story against the Aggies in Memorial since 1924 and said no jinx existed. Emory Bellard, of course, concurred.

Sports Illustrated had run a story on the Aggies with the title "Aggie Joke Is on Its Way Out." A&M cast doubt on that statement with three fumbles in the first quarter against Texas, one on the opening kickoff, one on its first play from scrimmage, and a third soon thereafter. Texas recovered and scored after all three for a 17–0 margin, which it expanded to 26–3 by intermission, when another coach in the series was honored. D. X.

Bubba Bean takes a pitchout from Mike Jay for a gain against the 'Horns, 1975.

Bible, now 83, was the only surviving member of the forty-three coaches who founded and attended the initial meeting of the American Football Coaches Association in New York in 1922. After another thirty minutes of football, Texas was the only surviving team on the field. Its 32–3 knockout of A&M paved the way for Baylor, which had come from behind to beat Texas two games before, to win its first conference title in fifty years and get mashed by Penn State in the Cotton Bowl. An 8–3 Texas team got to vacation at the Gator Bowl, where Auburn clawed it, 27–3. An 8–3 A&M team got to spend the holidays in College Station, Texas.

1975

"They're Sick. I Don't Like 'Em"

"To win any game, you have to basically outwit the opponents," wrote Dr. Gerard A. Donovan for *The Battalion*, "and for too long we have only half-heartedly met the Orange Balloon at Kyle Field and Memorial Stadium with the expected result: demolition."

In Texas' fifth game, the 'Horns put an unblemished season down before Oklahoma's Sooners, who had won thirty-three football

UT quarterback Marty Akins.

An injured Marty Akins is sacked by A&M defenders, 1975.

games in a row since bowing to Texas in 1972. A week before, Oklahoma's fans exhibited how such prosperity had warped their perspective. OU led Colorado 21–20 on that previous Saturday in Norman, Oklahoma, and the Sooner quarterback fell on the ball to preserve the win by running out the clock. The crowd booed. Oklahoma took Texas, 24–17, in Dallas for its fourth straight defeat of the hated school to the south. Texas A&M had never beaten Texas four games in a row. It hadn't beaten Texas three times in a row since 1909-10, and by the 1970s had

been reduced to praying for one in a row.

Coach Bellard, can you beat Texas? With a puff of his pipe, he answered, "If I said we would, you could say I was boasting. If I said we could not, I'd be telling a lie, so I reckon I'll say nothing. I will let the team speak for me on the field." Coaches never answer the question. At Kyle Field on the day after Thanksgiving, the nation's top offensive machine sputtered to ten points while the Aggies stacked up twenty, knotting the conference title three ways between A&M, Texas, and Arkansas. Texas' star quarterback, Marty

Akins, came into the game injured and retired after the first play, returning for only nine more during the contest. After their loss, Texas players pointed out that fact to reporters. Aggie linebacker Ed Simonini, who had angered Texas players with pre-game taunts, growled, "Man, if they say that was the difference, they're sick. I don't like 'em anyway." The feeling's mutual, Ed. Arkansas got the Cotton Bowl trip, relegating A&M to the Liberty, where Southern Cal bowled 'em over 20–0, and Texas picked the Bluebonnet, where they beat Colorado 38–21. ●

Tony Franklin increases A&M's lead over Texas by 3 in the 1975 A&M victory.

Ed Simonini lunges to haul down an opponent.

George Woodard (bottom of pile) *scores for A&M while quarterback David Walker signals a touchdown against UT, 1976.*

1976

A Very Good Aggie Year

Cadets jumped a railing at Memorial Stadium to fire "Old Smokey," Texas' cannon, when the Aggies scored. The game had been moved to the Saturday after Thanksgiving to facilitate the University of Houston's entry into the SWC. The score of A&M's second straight defeat of Texas—and its first victory at Austin since 1956—was 27–3. It was the worst beating Texas had taken at the hands of the Farmers since 1925. For the only time since 1939, Texas failed to score a touchdown against A&M.

If those statistical tidbits weren't enough to justify the Aggies' celebration long into the night, there were more. Texas' domination of Southwest Conference athletics throughout the league's history was incredible. Of fifty-eight football titles offered since 1915, the Longhorns had won outright or shared

twenty of them. Of the sixty handed out in baseball, Texas had forty-nine. It owned fifteen of the sixty-one basketball titles, thirty of fifty in golf, fourteen of thirty team titles in tennis, and had won thirty-six track championships from 1915 to 1976. The color of the Southwest Conference throne room had a definite orange tint.

Admittedly, the Aggies stood up to Texas' constant barrage better than most. Texas Tech had played SWC football seventeen years before it even tied for the title, and then it had the luck to tie with first-year member

Houston, which received the Cotton Bowl invitation because the Red Raiders had already been to that bowl (in 1939). Rice had won the basketball championship outright only four times, Baylor three. But when Texas A&M's winnings—thirteen track titles and nine each in football, basketball, and baseball were stacked up against Texas', the Aggies still came up considerably short. Not in 1976, though: the Aggies beat Texas in football, and won the conference basketball championship as well.

While A&M's fortunes were up, the University of Texas' were down. At 5–5–1, the school had its least successful football team in two decades. *The Texan* editorialized, "It might be an appropriate time to propose disassembly of this hulking semi-professional apparatus which dominates all other athletic endeavors."

1977

Such Good Friends

Is it worth spending two days in line for a football ticket? "Against A&M it is," said one Texas student. "I've got to say that I can't stand Texas A&M." He was among 1,200 in line at the UT ticket offices when they opened Monday morning; many had been there since Saturday. The game, after all, did promise to be a good one. Texas, with the invincible Earl Campbell at running back, was the country's No. 1 team at 10–0. A&M was rated No. 12 after winning seven of nine games. George Woodard, described as Texas A&M's version of the World Trade Center, slimmed down from 286 to 255 pounds for the occasion. Emory Bellard had been criticized, amaz-

ingly, for still running the "dead" wishbone, although A&M led the U.S. in rushing. Bellard had been on the Texas staff with Fred Akers, who in 1977 took over after Darrell Royal retired from coaching with a 109–72–2 record, one of the best at a school that demands success.

Bellard and Akers were asked if they had been good friends while working together under Royal or if they were just on the staff together. Bellard said, "I'd like to think we were good friends although I don't know what Freddie would say." Freddie said, "We were on the staff together."

Again, traditions clashed. A Texas student group had a practice of unfurling a huge state flag on the field before games. But A&M considered its field a memorial to A&M's war dead, and tradition allowed only yell leaders and football players onto the playing surface

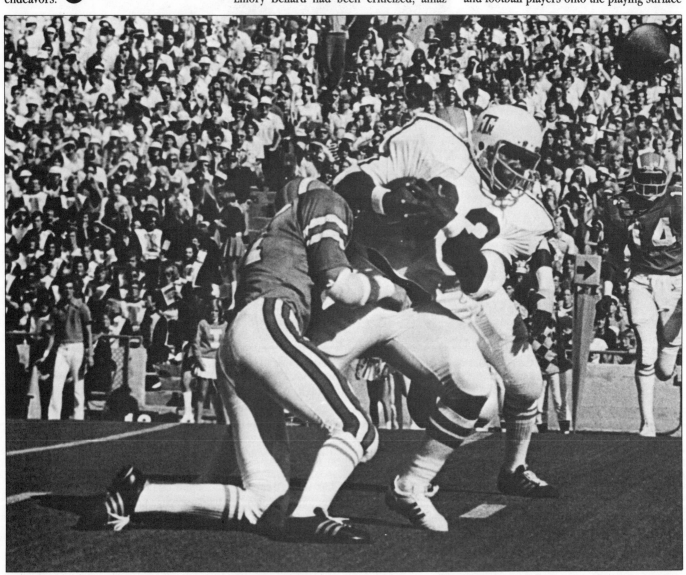

George Woodard fights for yardage in the 1977 Aggie victory over Illinois. Woodard led the Southwest Conference in scoring during the 1976 season.

Halfback Curtis Dickey romps for a gain as UT's Johnnie Johnson is taken out of the play, 1977.

Glen Blackwood is shoved out of bounds by Aggie defenders during the 1977 A&M-UT contest.

before a contest. The Texas band, a spirit group called the Cowboys, and the Austin flag-bearers all thought they had an understanding with A&M's yell leaders. But when the band started playing "The Eyes of Texas" and some UT students rushed onto the field, corps members swarmed from all sides to suggest they leave. After the field was cleared, the flag-carriers emerged and the cadets quickly beset them and ushered them away as well, with only one fistfight erupting.

In the official battle minutes later, Campbell rushed for 222 yards and three touchdowns and Woodard topped 1,000 yards for his season. Aggie defensive end Phil Bennett said, "If Campbell doesn't get the Heisman, they should throw the damn trophy away." Bellard said, "He is the best running back I have ever seen." The Longhorns became the first team to notch eight SWC victories in a season with their 57–28 triumph, completing their regular season undefeated before that familiar bully, Notre Dame, mugged them in the Cotton Bowl, 38–10. The Aggies won their eighth game a week later over Houston, then met Southern Cal in the Bluebonnet Bowl, where USC won, 47–28. 🏈

Aggie halfback David Brothers takes a breather during the UT game, 1977.

In 1977, A&M head coach Emory Bellard was criticized for continuing to run the "dead" wishbone, despite his team's national lead in rushing yardage.

UT's Earl Campbell shows his Heisman Trophy—winning style.

UT's Fred Akers meets A&M's Emory Bellard at mid-field after Texas' 57–28 drubbing of A&M, 1977.

1978

"Nothing Else Matters"

Texas kicker Russell Erxleben said, "A lot of people talk about the OU rivalry, but I like this one [with A&M] better. Oklahoma is up there and you don't see those people but once a year. You have to see Aggies all the time." Erxleben and Aggie Tony Franklin were the league's best kickers, and had a friendly rivalry going on their own. Erxleben added, "When I look back at this game, I want to be able to say, 'I went out a winner and I did it against A&M.'"

The Aggies bombed their first four opponents by an average score of 43–5, but when they lost their fifth and sixth games (33–0 to Houston and 24–6 to Baylor), Emory Bellard resigned under intense pressure. Nobody ever said alumni have level heads. Assistant Tom Wilson was promoted to head coach and achieved the same 4–2 record for his mini-season that Bellard had for his six games. Half of Wilson's losses came at the hands of Texas, 22–7, however, and already some A&M supporters didn't like him. He took his Aggies to the Hall of Fame Bowl where they beat Iowa State 28–12, but Bellard probably could have done that.

There was disappointment in Austin, too, where Fred Akers hadn't done himself any favors by going 11–1 his rookie year. His 1978 record of 8–3 didn't look good in comparison, and it included losses to Oklahoma (the winningest team of the 1970s) and Baylor, plus league champ Houston. The 42–0 job the Steers did on Maryland in the Sun Bowl saved the wounds some, and at least the 'Horns beat A&M. Wilson was asked before the game about the importance of the A&M-Texas match. He said, "We're Texas A&M and they're Texas fixin' to line up and play football and nothing else matters."

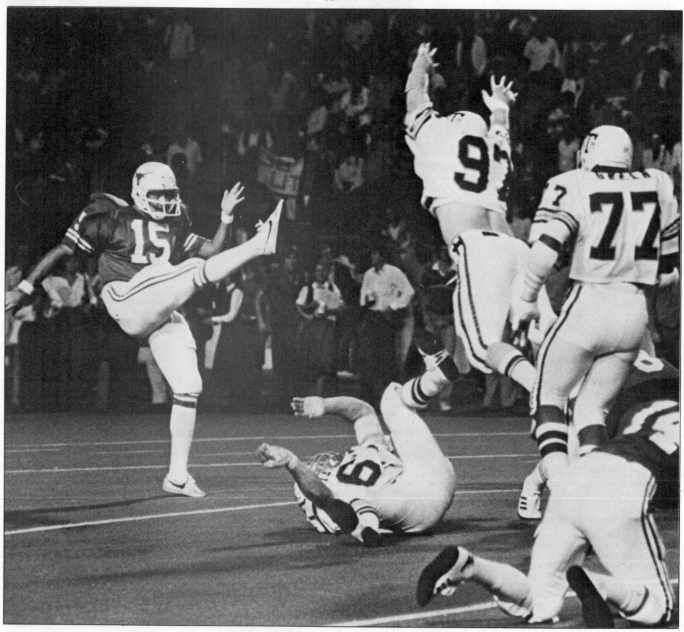

"A lot of people talk about the OU rivalry, but I like this one better." Russell Erxleben's punt clears the Aggie rush, 1978.

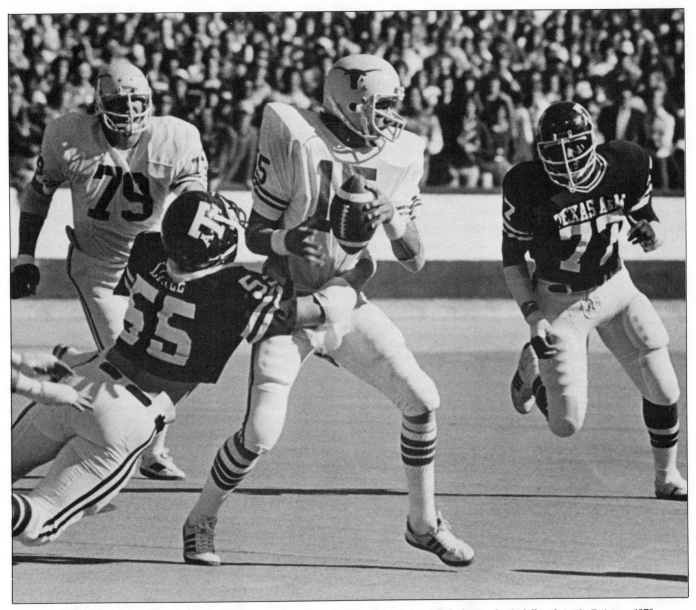

Rick McIvor feels the pressure of the Aggie rush as A&M's Mike Little (55) and Jacob Green (77) close in for the kill in their 13–7 victory, 1979.

1979

"Ten Times Better"

Texas' Leroy King said, "I'd rather lose to TCU or Rice." It didn't work that way for Leroy and his teammates in 1979, however. Tom Wilson's Aggies opened their season with losses to Brigham Young and Baylor, but appeared to be on the winning track after an upset of Penn State on the road. Still, approaching its eleventh game, what some had thought was a potential 11–0 A&M squad was mired at 5–5. Among other strangeness, someone stole A&M's game plans for the Texas Tech game and sent them to Red

Raider coach Rex Dockery, who returned them immediately. "Beating Texas would make us feel a little better," Wilson said.

By game day, Texas and A&M students had come to an agreement about the pre-game restrictions on Kyle Field. The cadets allowed Texas' cannon and drum onto the field, and even Bevo. But the huge Texas flag was barred. The Capital City A&M Club had complained about KVUE-TV's Aggie Jokes Contest (even though Texas jokes were allowed), and Texas fans disagreed over the now-popular use of the words *eat shit* in "Texas Fight."

Texas fumbled four kicks, a share of the SWC crown, and a Sugar Bowl berth in A&M's 13–7 upset victory; its holiday foe trans-

formed from Alabama to Washington (in the Sun Bowl). The Aggies had a winning season at 6–5, but only the defeat of Texas made the potentially great year seem profitable. Wilson was given a new contract through 1982. "This is ten times better than Penn State," A&M quarterback Mike Mosley giggled after the game. Fred Akers faced his quarterback, Rick McIvor, after the setback and told him, "You have three more opportunities [to beat A&M]. Don't you forget this one." Upon arrival in El Paso for the Sun Bowl, John Goodson, Texas kicker, said, "Well, it's better than College Station." It wasn't much better, as Texas followed one upset loss with another, 14–7, to the Washington Huskies.

1980

Ninety-four Years to Go

"They just humiliated us [last year]," said Texas tackle Steve Massey. "They embarrassed us in every phase. They probably also think we're ripe for another upset. But we're not." Center David Bandy offered the Aggies' viewpoint: "We had 15,000 Aggies standing out in the snow at the bonfire. . . . You can tell the Longhorns they'd better be ready. We'll be there." Things did not look good for the Farmers. Tom Wilson was under fire for his team's 3–7 year, which included a drug scandal that forced Wilson to put two starters off the team. The experts thought a loss to Texas surely would be the boot that would kick Wilson out. *American-Statesman* columnist Bill Sullivan theorized, "All of a sudden, ol' Emory doesn't seem like such a bad guy, and who ever said the wishbone was

dull?" Bellard, by the way, had taken up residence at Mississippi State and engineered an upset of Alabama, which hadn't lost a game virtually since footballs became pointed. Wilson was feeling the pressure that had finally squeezed Bellard out of College Station. Bandy thought: "There's just too much pressure. Why? Because we always get beat by Texas. I felt pretty good about winning last year. It's a lot better than losing but Texas is up with 60 wins, and we've won 21. That's ridiculous."

During the spring of 1980, Texas alumni received a brochure with a picture of an Aggie on the front. Cadet Dean Bernal had been caught with a look of only semi-intelligence while whooping it up at the A&M-Rice game of 1979, and his photo was used for the UT pamphlet under the legend, "Will the 'Horns become an Aggie joke?" Inside, UT grads were urged to contribute generously to their school. "We can beat those Aggies at football, basketball and in academic areas. But when it comes to alumni support, they have us whipped." Aggies bristled, but H. C. "Dulie"

Bell of Austin, a Texas A&M board member, called the brochure good publicity. "It gives A&M incentive to do even better."

The Aggies did better in the football game, by 24–14, and Texas was left holding its third "upset" loss of the season. Texas Tech had beaten an undefeated Longhorn squad, then SMU won in Austin, and Texas also lost to SWC champ Baylor. Tying for fourth place with Rice at 4–4 turned a lot of Texas fans' faces red. "There was poor play calling," whined one disgruntled Orange rooter after the "miserable" 7–4 regular season. "They just don't have any zip. This game, the SMU game, the Tech game. . . . I just don't understand it," said another. "You're damn right," said a fan when a reporter asked him if people were unhappy with Akers. "In four years, he hasn't produced an offensive football team." Through it all, Tom Wilson smiled, even cried. A&M had, for the second time in six years, beaten Texas two years in a row. If the Aggies kept that up, the series would be even in ninety-four years. ⬤

Mike Mosley (11), Darrell Adams (47), and Reveille bowl for victory before the 1980 UT game.

The building of the Aggie bonfire is supervised by "redpots" (in helmets), *a much coveted position. The center pole construction was used for the first time in 1946.*

A pensive Roosevelt Leaks watches from the UT bench, 1972. Leaks was a 1973 All-America and All- Southwest Conference selection.

A&M players Carl Roaches, Pat Thomas, and Jackie Williams pose off-field.

The Aggie crowd, standing by as the Twelfth Man, gives strong vocal support to their team from the stands, 1973.

All-Southwest Conference safety Dave Elmendorf lettered at A&M from 1968 to 1970.

The final score tells it all, 1975.

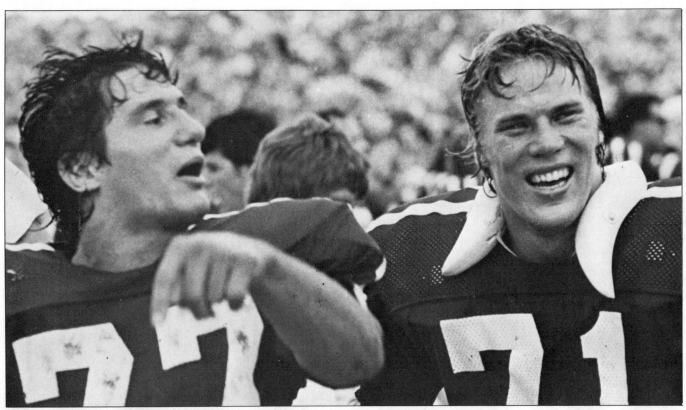

All-Southwest Conference linebacker Ed Simonini (77) joins with Garth Ten Napel to taunt tea-sips.

UT quarterback Donnie Little scrambles for a gain, 1980.

A Battalion *cartoon celebrates the end of the 1980 football season.*

The outhouse for the 1977 Aggie bonfire reflects College Station's sentiment concerning Earl Campbell.

Mark Lewis is congratulated by fellow Aggie teammates after a touchdown catch awards Farmers their second consecutive victory over UT, 24–14.

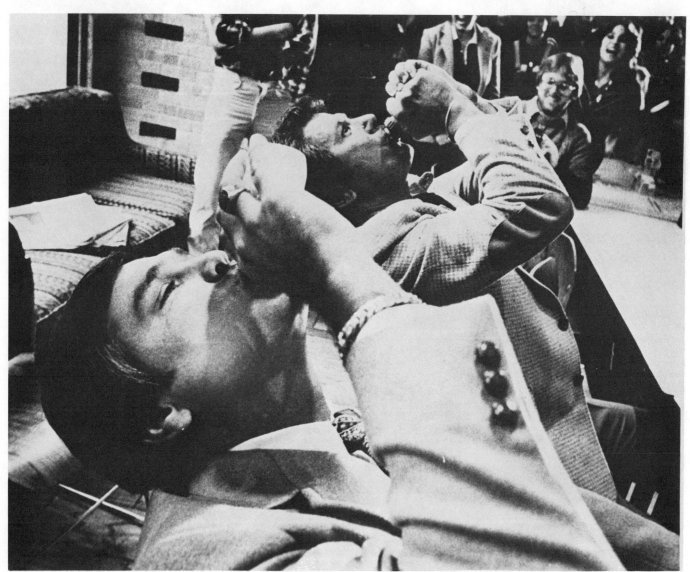

"T is for Texas U? Hellno! T is for Tea-Sippers!" One version of the Aggie War Hymn makes reference to the "favorite activity" of UT's "country club" members. A&M coach Tom Wilson and Athletic Director Marvin Tate compete in a tea-sipping contest.

1894–1980

Year	Winner	Score	Site
1894	Texas	38–0	Austin
1898	Texas	48–0	Austin
1899	Texas	6–0	San Antonio
1900	Texas	5–0	San Antonio
	Texas	11–0	Austin
1901	Texas	17–0	San Antonio
	Texas	32–0	Austin
1902	Tie	0–0	San Antonio
	A&M	11–0	Austin
1903	Texas	29–6	Austin
1904	Texas	34–6	Austin
1905	Texas	27–0	Austin
1906	Texas	24–0	Austin
1907	Tie	0–0	Dallas
	Texas	11–6	Austin
1908	Texas	24–8	Houston
	Texas	28–12	Austin
1909	A&M	23–0	Houston
	A&M	5–0	Austin
1910	A&M	14–8	Houston
1911	Texas	6–0	Houston
1915	A&M	13–0	College Station
1916	Texas	21–7	Austin
1917	A&M	7–0	College Station
1918	Texas	7–0	Austin
1919	A&M	7–0	College Station
1920	Texas	7–3	Austin
1921	Tie	0–0	College Station
1922	A&M	14–7	Austin
1923	Texas	6–0	College Station
1924	Texas	7–0	Austin
1925	A&M	28–0	College Station
1926	Texas	14–5	Austin
1927	A&M	28–7	College Station
1928	Texas	19–0	Austin
1929	A&M	13–0	College Station
1930	Texas	26–0	Austin
1931	A&M	7–6	College Station
1932	Texas	21–0	Austin
1933	Tie	10–10	College Station
1934	Texas	13–0	Austin
1935	A&M	20–6	College Station
1936	Texas	7–0	Austin
1937	A&M	7–0	College Station
1938	Texas	7–6	Austin
1939	A&M	20–0	College Station
1940	Texas	7–0	Austin
1941	Texas	23–0	College Station

1942	Texas	12–6	Austin
1943	Texas	27–13	College Station
1944	Texas	6–0	Austin
1945	Texas	20–10	College Station
1946	Texas	24–7	Austin
1947	Texas	32–13	College Station
1948	Tie	14–14	Austin
1949	Texas	42–14	College Station
1950	Texas	17–0	Austin
1951	A&M	22–21	College Station
1952	Texas	32–12	Austin
1953	Texas	21–12	College Station
1954	Texas	22–13	Austin
1955	Texas	21–6	College Station
1956	A&M	34–21	Austin
1957	Texas	9–7	College Station
1958	Texas	27–0	Austin
1959	Texas	20–17	College Station
1960	Texas	21–14	Austin
1961	Texas	25–0	College Station
1962	Texas	13–3	Austin
1963	Texas	15–13	College Station
1964	Texas	26–7	Austin
1965	Texas	21–17	College Station
1966	Texas	22–14	Austin
1967	A&M	10–7	College Station
1968	Texas	35–14	Austin
1969	Texas	49–12	College Station
1970	Texas	52–14	Austin
1971	Texas	34–14	College Station
1972	Texas	38–3	Austin
1973	Texas	42–13	College Station
1974	Texas	32–3	Austin
1975	A&M	20–10	College Station
1976	A&M	27–3	Austin
1977	Texas	57–28	College Station
1978	Texas	22–7	Austin
1979	A&M	13–7	College Station
1980	A&M	24–14	Austin

Texas wins: 60
A&M wins: 22
Ties: 5

Bibliography

Berry, Margaret Catherine. *UT Austin—Traditions and Nostalgia*. Austin, Texas: Shoal Creek Publishers, Inc., 1975.

Cohane, Tim. *Great College Football Coaches of the Twenties and Thirties*. New Rochelle, N.Y.: Arlington House, 1973.

Evans, Wilbur, and McElroy, H. B. *The Twelfth Man*. Huntsville, Alabama: Strode Publishers, Inc., 1975.

Freeman, Denne H. *Hook 'em Horns: A Story of Texas Football*. Huntsville, Alabama: Strode Publishers, 1974.

Kaye, Ivan N. *Good Clean Violence: A History of College Football*. New York: J. P. Lippincott Co., 1973.

Maysel, Lou. *Here Come the Longhorns:* 2 vols. Austin, Texas: Burnt Orange Publishing, 1978.

Morris, Willie. *North Toward Home*. New York: Dell Publishing Co., Inc., 1967.

Tips, Kern. *Football—Texas Style*. Garden City, N.Y.: Doubleday & Co., Inc., 1964.

Photo Credits